Writers of Wales

EDITORS

MEIC STEPHENS   R. BRINLEY JONES

Title Page of 'Silex Scintillans'

By courtesy of the Bodleian Library

Alan Rudrum

HENRY VAUGHAN

University of Wales Press
on behalf of the Welsh Arts Council

1981

Henry Vaughan and his twin brother Thomas were born at Newton-upon-Usk, Breconshire, in 1621. Henry was the elder twin. They were probably the oldest surviving children of Thomas Vaughan of Tretower and Denise Morgan. Henry Vaughan's biographer, F. E. Hutchinson, who worked from notes compiled by Louise Imogen Guiney and Gwenllian E. F. Morgan, was not able to establish with certainty many dates relating to the Vaughans' early years; but we may say that their brother William was probably born in 1628 and that by 1632 both Henry and Thomas were living at Llangattock under the tuition of Matthew Herbert. Vaughan was to look back upon Herbert's tuition with great respect. In the Latin poem 'Ad Posteros' *(To Posterity)* prefixed to Olor Iscanus, he wrote:

Wales gave me birth, in the place where Father Usk launches down from the windswept mountains to wander in broad valleys. Then Herbert, a man most expert in learning, the master of Latin scholarship, took me under his serene protection, and under his guidance I progressed for six years. This one man bestowed a double bounty: learning and love.

(Poems, p. 63).

Near the end of Olor Iscanus there is a short Latin poem addressed to Matthew Herbert, in the title of which Vaughan describes him as *formerly his tutor and always his most cherished friend* and in which he gives Herbert credit for the fame that will be his after death (POEMS, p. 131). Thomas Vaughan too expressed gratitude to Herbert, addressing to him two Latin poems and the Epistle Dedicatory of his polemical work THE MAN-MOUSE. Of course the compliment to an old schoolmaster amounts to a minor poetic *genre* in the Renaissance; but the fact that the Vaughan twins both adopted it is itself significant.

Thomas Vaughan was admitted into Jesus College, Oxford (traditionally the college for Welshmen) on 4 May, 1638, and matriculated on 14 December of the same year. It has been assumed that both young men entered Oxford at the same time; but there is no formal record of Henry's residence there. It may be that, intending from the first not to take a degree, he economized by not matriculating. The Buttery-Books of Jesus College show that Thomas was billed for larger amounts than the average, which may suggest that the twins were billed together. However, Thomas's bills continued large after Henry is presumed to have left Oxford for London to study law, probably in 1640. While the official record is silent, Henry Vaughan wrote to the biographer John Aubrey in 1673: *I stayed not at Oxford to take any degree, but was sent to London, being then designed by my father for the study of the Law, which the sudden eruption of our late civil wars wholly frustrated* (M 763). This certainly suggests that Henry did reside in Oxford for a while, which is what one would expect to have happened in the normal course of events. So does the fact that the information supplied to Aubrey was used in Anthony Wood's Oxford history (HISTORIA ET ANTIQUITATES

Universitatis Oxoniensis, 1674) for the lives of Thomas and Henry Vaughan. Disappointingly, there is no official evidence of Vaughan's formal education. There are no records of his presumed period in the Inns of Court (a common phenomenon: we know that Cromwell was there but there is no official record); and we do not know when or where he took a degree in medicine, which was it seems his livelihood for a great part of his adult life. In a letter to Aubrey (15 June, 1673; M 687–9) he explains that he is writing from Brecon, where *I am still attending our Bishop's Lady in a tertian fever;* at the end of the letter, having explained that Thomas's *employment was in physic and chemistry* he adds *My profession also is physic, which I have practised now for many years with good success (I thank God!) and a repute big enough for a person of greater parts than myself.* Twenty years later, in a letter written two years before his death, he describes himself as being engaged *with Mr. Serjeant Le Hunt's Lady, who is most dangerously sick in a putrid fever with most malignant symptoms.*

It is clear that Henry Vaughan was given the education of a gentleman of his time and place; that is, he read the Latin classics, and at some point acquired some Greek—how much is uncertain. While his major publications are all in English, it is likely that he grew up speaking Welsh, and that while staying with Matthew Herbert he and Thomas acquired a knowledge of Welsh legend and poetry. In 'Daphnis', an elegaic eclogue probably written originally for his brother William in 1648 and adapted after the death of Thomas in 1666, he writes:

Here, when the careless world did sleep, have I
In dark records and numbers nobly high
The visions of our black, but brightest bard
From old Amphion's *mouth full often heard.*

Here it is likely that 'Amphion' is Matthew Herbert, and the 'black, but brightest bard' may be Myrddin Emrys (Merlin Ambrosius), on whom see the note on line 61 in POEMS. However, apart from a few lines, thought to be by Henry, in Thomas Powell's CERBYD JECHYDWRIAETH *(Chariot of Salvation)* I know of no writing by him in Welsh; there is certainly some Welsh influence in his verse (his occasional use of Welsh gender for example); but its exact nature and extent remains to be investigated.

The fact that Henry and Thomas were both strongly interested in 'hermetic philosophy' suggests that it may well have been Matthew Herbert who initiated them into the works of 'Hermes Trismegistus', the ORACLES of Zoroaster, and such anthologies of hermetic and alchemical lore as the THEATRUM CHEMICUM, the HERMETIC MUSEUM, Henry Cornelius Agrippa's DE OCCULTA PHILOSOPHIA, and the multifarious works attributed to Paracelsus. If so, then it follows that their acquaintance with the literature of hermeticism began earlier than the 1640s, when the religious ferment associated with the Civil War gave rise to a vast number of 'heresies', many of which appear to have roots in hermeticism, to judge by their characterisation in Thomas Edwards' GANGRAENA (1646). Such early acquaintance would go some way to explain what otherwise might seem rather odd, namely the fact that the Vaughan twins should have been staunch members of the Church of England and yet exhibit such sympathy with a range of unorthodoxies which during the Civil troubles were adopted by the extreme left wing of their political and religious enemies. Generally speaking it was the sectaries rather than the Anglicans who adopted hermetic ideas.

Except for THALIA REDIVIVA, published in 1678 but containing work written much earlier, all of Henry Vaughan's publications appeared during the Civil War and Interregnum, between 1646 and 1657. The careful reader of his work cannot help but become aware of the pain he felt during the troubles of that time; and it seems reasonable to suggest that much of his work springs from an attempt to retain equilibrium during what he experienced as persecution.

Vaughan was probably in London in the early 1640s, when the country was running headlong towards civil conflict. He may have witnessed the London mob calling for the head of Strafford (there seems to be an allusion to this in his translation of Juvenal: see POEMS 57, lines 440–1 and note). In this work and in several poems in OLOR ISCANUS, one senses Vaughan's feelings of personal involvement in the civil disturbances. The delayed publication of OLOR ISCANUS (of which the preface is dated 1647) may have been due to the need to omit a number of poems too indiscreetly partisan for the publisher's comfort, and to substitute a number of poems written after 1647. In the religious poems of SILEX SCINTILLANS, direct reference is comparatively rare; nevertheless Vaughan's Royalist sympathies

—and indignation—would be clear enough in SILEX even if other evidence were lacking. The frequent apocalyptic references in SILEX are understandable enough if we remember that through virtually all his career as a writer Vaughan must have expected to live under a Puritan republican régime for the rest of his days. This represented for him a wilderness in religion and in politics; outside the sphere of the immediately personal, he could only look for comfort to the Last Judgement.

It seems likely that the Civil War touched Henry very personally. There is circumstantial evidence that he fought in it himself; and it seems likely that the death of his brother William (mourned in a number of beautiful elegies) was caused by wounds or privations suffered in the war. In the Preface to THE MAN-MOUSE, Thomas Vaughan speaks of William as having died *upon a . . . glorious employment,* and in THE MOUNT OF OLIVES Henry writes of his enemies that they had *washed their hands in the blood* of his *dearest and nearest relatives* (M 167). I am inclined to ascribe his turning almost exclusively to religious verse (that is, what is often called his 'conversion') to his grief at the death of William (1648), his shock at the execution of Charles I (1649), and perhaps to an illness which he is known to have suffered. In the Preface to the 1655 SILEX he describes himself as a convert of 'Mr. George Herbert'; certainly by the time he came to write SILEX he had undergone a period of immersion in the poems of Herbert and in the Bible.

Very little is known of the details of Vaughan's life after he returned to live at Newton-upon-

Usk. Aubrey says that *he was a clerk sometime to Judge Sir Marmaduke Lloyd,* who was an active royalist and discharged from his office as judge in 1645. As Hutchinson suggests, Vaughan's period as a minor legal official can hardly have lasted longer than from 1642–1645 (LIFE 49). We do not know when he began to practise medicine, but such prose works as HERMETICAL PHYSIC (1655) and THE CHEMIST'S KEY (1657), as well as medical references in SILEX SCINTILLANS, suggest that he was studying medicine, if not already practising, during the 1650s. His later life must have been saddened by disagreements with the children of his first marriage, recorded in the LIFE, but these are of no special interest to a reader of the poems. In 1689 Vaughan left the house at Newton, where he had spent the greater part of his life, yielding occupancy to his elder son, and moving with his wife Elizabeth to a cottage at Scethrog. The lintel-stone of the cottage, bearing the inscription H^{V}E 1689, is now at the foot of Vaughan's gravestone in the churchyard at Llansantffraed. The fact that Vaughan was buried in the churchyard rather than in the church, which would have been more usual at that time for a person of his social standing, was probably intended to symbolise humility rather than love of nature. Under the family coat of arms, the gravestone, by Vaughan's own wish, bears the words

SERVUS INUTILIS:
PECCATOR MAXIMUS

(Unprofitable servant: greatest of sinners).

Sitting by his grave, one can hear the sound he loved so well, the running waters of the Usk.

Secular Poems

Henry Vaughan's first volume of verse, POEMS, WITH THE TENTH SATIRE OF JUVENAL ENGLISHED, appeared in 1646. The Civil War had been in progress for four years, and Vaughan had by then probably seen military service. Whatever troubles he may have experienced up to that time, two were in the future: the death of a beloved younger brother, William, in 1648, and the execution of Charles I on the scaffold in 1649.

The original poems of POEMS 1646 are such as might have been expected from a very young man at that time. His own maturation, his falling in love, his literary attachments and ambitions, are what chiefly interest him. The outside world was threatening, ugly, provocative of scorn; but events had not yet gathered into the storm that was to sweep away Vaughan's youthful pre-occupations. Nevertheless the consciousness of that outside world is there, exerting some pressure. In the Preface to the volume he appeals to those *whose more refined spirits out-wing these dull times, and soar above the drudgeries of dirty intelligence* (that is, news of current political events). In reference to his Juvenal translation, he describes the Roman author as one whose pen *had as much true passion, for the infirmities of that state, as we should have pity, to the distractions of our own.* He hints darkly at topical application; it cannot be offensive, he says, except to those who will *purposely arraign themselves. These indeed may think, that they have slept out so many centuries in this satire, and are now awaked; which, had it been still Latin, perhaps their nap had been everlasting* —a neatly delivered suggestion that his enemies were unlettered as well as rebellious.

There are fourteen poems in POEMS 1646. The first is addressed to a friend; the next eight are love-poems; the tenth is a tavern-poem; the eleventh and twelfth continue the sequence to Amoret; the thirteenth is about a place, the Priory Grove at Brecon, hallowed by association with her; the last is the long and loose translation of Juvenal's tenth satire. It would not be altogether unfair to dismiss the volume as the work of a young man with no very clear voice of his own and not much to say. There is a certain youthful self-consciousness in the attempt to project a *persona:* the Vaughan who addressed his 'ingenuous friend R.W.' would be seen as a spendthrift tavern-haunter, and 'A Rhapsody' is in one aspect a splendid celebration of the seamier side of London life. The love-poems abound with echoes of Habington's CASTARA, and the echo of Donne in the third and fourth stanzas of 'To Amoret of the difference 'twixt him, and other lovers, and what true love is,' is quite blatant. Nevertheless the volume is not without interest; on the one hand we find, lightly handled, themes and interests that will deepen and take on greater resonance in SILEX SCINTILLANS (the theme of the restoration of all things, for example, in 'To my ingenuous friend, R.W.' and in 'Upon the Priory Grove'). On the other hand, some of the more successful poems in this volume differ so markedly in manner from Vaughan's mature poetry as to suggest that our gain in SILEX SCINTILLANS was bought at a price. Consider for example lines 35–46 of 'A Rhapsody':

Should we go now a wandering, we should meet
With catchpoles, whores, & carts in every street:

Now when each narrow lane, each nook & cave,
Sign-posts, & shop-doors, pimp for every knave,
When riotous sinful plush, and tell-tale spurs
Walk Fleet street, & the Strand, when the soft stirs
Of bawdy, ruffled silks, turn night to day;
And the loud whip, and coach scolds all the way;
When lust of all sorts, and each itchy blood
From the Tower-wharf to Cymbeline, and Lud,
Hunts for a mate, and the tired footman reels
'Twixt chair-men, torches, & the hackney wheels.

This is unlike anything we find in SILEX SCINTILLANS, and suggests that Vaughan used his eyes and imagination to some purpose during his period in London. On the face of it straightforwardly descriptive, it is not without art. As Donne in the first stanza of 'The Canonization', by linking several nouns to each verb, suggests the multiplicity of possible choices, so here Vaughan suggests the sinister and bewildering variety of the scene: *we should meet/With catchpoles, whores, & carts* and *each narrow lane, each nook & cave,/ Sign-posts, & shop-doors, pimp for every knave*. In the second of these examples, the personification of the objects named, implicit in making them the subject of 'pimp' (Marilla's gloss is inaccurate), adds force to that verb, already energized as the successively-named subjects stretch the spring of the reader's expectations. The association of luxury and lechery is nicely suggested by the attribution of moral qualities to the inanimate, as in 'riotous sinful plush' and 'bawdy, ruffled silks'. It is a passage, such as we find in Spenser and Milton, in which the attraction of what is forbidden is evoked in the same moment as it is morally 'placed'. In its evocation of the bustle of city life, it has more in common with the London-based dramatists of a slightly earlier time than with the 'Silurist' of a slightly later one. So too has the passage in 'To Amoret Weeping' (also in the context of a conditional statement) from lines 27–36:

I should perhaps eat orphans, and suck up
A dozen distressed widows in one cup;
Nay further, I should by that lawful stealth,
(Damned usury) undo the Common-wealth;
Or patent it in soap, and coals, and so
Have the smiths curse me, and my laundress too;
Geld wine, or his friend tobacco; and so bring
The incensed subject rebel to his king;
And after all (as those first sinners fell)
Sink lower than my gold; and lie in hell.

This may (I don't know) be directly plagiarized from one of the Jacobean dramatists; it certainly captures their manner, their concreteness of moral perception, very well.

Vaughan had spent only a short time in London; but it was as Hutchinson says a time when critical events followed one another in close succession. Vaughan's excited interest in politics is quite clear from 'A Rhapsody', where a toast is proposed *to him/That made his horse a Senator* (which must surely have been read as a contemptuous reference to Parliament); another to *he! that like fire broke forth/Into the Senate's face, crossed Rubicon . . . And made the dull gray beards, & furred gowns fly* (a reference to Julius Caesar which must have been interpreted in terms of Charles I's attempt to arrest the five members in January 1641–2); and another to 'brave Sylla', who had for Vaughan this much in common with Strafford, that he could be seen as upholder of the patricians against the *populares.* E. L. Marilla's dogmatic assertion that *Vaughan intends no parallel allusion here to men of his own time* surely represents an over-determined attempt to reject received opinion. A string of allusions that *could* be read as veiled commentary on recent political events surely *would* have been so read by anyone with the (not very profound) classical learning required to perceive the similarities; and the device of employing historical allusions in this way is a time-honoured method of having one's say and keeping one's skin intact in difficult circumstances.

This is not to say that it is always easy for us to pick up the significance of such allusions. No amount of reading can make us Vaughan's contemporaries, and few of us have a knowledge of the classics and of ancient history as ready as theirs. For my part I have only one suggestion to add to those of Louise Guiney, Gwenllian Morgan, and F. E. Hutchinson. In lines 440–2 of the Juvenal translation, Vaughan writes, in reference to Pompey, *our public vows/Made* Caesar *guiltless; but sent him to lose/His head at Nile.* The relevant passage in Juvenal is lines 283–6 *(provida Pompeio . . . caput abstulit)* which Loeb translates: *Kindly Campania gave to Pompey a fever, which he might have prayed for us as a boon; but the public prayers of all those cities gained the day; so his own fortune and that of Rome preserved him to be vanquished and to lose his head.* There is nothing in Juvenal to warrant Vaughan's words; he is probably referring to the clamour for the execution of the Earl of Strafford, and the part Charles played in signing his death-warrant. The word 'our' has no warrant in the original *(publica vota)* and would have signalled to an alert contemporary that a modern allusion was intended. Strafford was executed on Tower Hill in 1641. Vaughan's 'translation' was of course published three years before Charles was executed and it may be doubted whether, after 1649, Vaughan would have referred to the part the king played in Strafford's downfall—it is painful to romantic Royalists to this day.

There has been a good deal of discussion about why Olor Iscanus, the dedication of which is dated from *Newton by Usk this 17. of December 1647,* was not published until 1651, the year after the first part of Silex Scintillans; and why the title-page declares it as being *published by a friend.* One view, already mentioned, is that the delay, and the composition of the volume as actually published, was dictated by political considerations, and that poems concerned with politics and the Civil War were edited out. Another view is that Vaughan came to disapprove of amorous verse; and that publication was delayed while Vaughan was removing such poems. The weakness of this theory, it seems to me, is that a poet who has set his face against amorous verses scarcely requires years to delete them; nor would a poet and verse-translator as prolific as Vaughan require years to fill a volume thinned by such editing out. A related, more positive suggestion is that Vaughan began to write the poems which were to appear in the first part of Silex Scintillans and rather lost interest in those assembled for OLOR ISCANUS. It is doubtful if certainty can be reached, but I incline to the view that publication was delayed, and some poems suppressed, for political reasons. Vaughan was an outspoken man, as is obvious from many passages in his poems and prose translations; a publisher might well have hesitated to endanger himself by dealing in poems which represented a continuation of hostilities. There is an indicated *hiatus* near the end of 'An Epitaph upon the Lady Elizabeth, second daughter of his late Majesty', which suggests that the occasion got the better of Vaughan in a way his publisher couldn't condone. Then there is the commendatory poem by Thomas Powell, prefaced to THALIA REDIVIVA (1678) but clearly written originally for an earlier collection. Here Vaughan is compared to *brave* Tyrtaeus, who *as we read of old,/The* Grecian *armies, as he pleased could* mold;/*They marched to his high* numbers, *and did fight/With that instinct and rage, which he did write.* This suggests that poems were suppressed from the originally-projected OLOR ISCANUS which did not eventually find a place in THALIA REDIVIVA. If Thomas Powell played an important part in the preparation of OLOR ISCANUS for publication, as has been suggested (and it seems likely) he might well have argued his younger friend into greater discretion, suggesting that while Vaughan was under a moral obligation not to assist the Parliamentary régime (that he was later asked to and refused seems almost certain from 'The Proffer' in SILEX II), he was under no moral obligation to bring difficulties upon himself and his family by trying to publish 'seditious' utterances.

The view that the suppressed poems were political rather than amorous seems rather more plausible when we recall how many of Vaughan's friends were uncompromising Royalists and Anglicans. Powell himself was evicted from his living in 1650, was causing the authorities a good deal of trouble in 1653 (see Hutchinson's chapter 'The Puritan Régime') and may subsequently have been imprisoned and then forced to go overseas. Matthew Herbert, who had tutored the Vaughan twins at Llangattock, was displaced in 1646, but continued to preach, apparently until 1655. In that year he even had the gaiety of spirit to sue some of his parishioners for non-payment of tithes! In 1656 he spent seventeen weeks in Brecon jail and was threatened with banishment. Thomas Lewes, rector of Llanfigan, to whom a poem in OLOR ISCANUS was addressed, was also displaced, and combined with Powell in resisting the authorities: see their defiant letter to Jenkin Jones (LIFE, page 119).

OLOR ISCANUS contains more translations than original poems; many of them are from Boethius' CONSOLATION OF PHILOSOPHY and from the Polish Jesuit neo-Latin poet Casimir Sarbiewski. These are likely to belong to the period when Vaughan was beginning to turn to exclusively religious themes; and that he should translate the work of a Jesuit bears witness to his oecumenical spirit, so ably discussed by Canon A. M. Allchin in an address given at the 1975 Vaughan Memorial Service at Llansantffraed. Several of the others are on literary themes; for example, 'Upon Mr. Fletcher's Plays'; 'Upon the Poems and Plays of the ever memorable Mr. William Cartwright';

'To Sir William Davenant upon his Gondibert'. There are two fine elegies, 'On the Death of Mr. R.W., slain . . . at Rowton Heath' and 'On the Death of Mr. R. Hall, slain at Pontefract'.

On the title-page Vaughan is described as 'Silurist' and the volume is prefaced by an adaptation from Virgil's second Georgic: 'O quis me gelidis in vallibus ISCAE/Sistat' *(O who will set me in the cool valleys of the Usk?)*. There is less attention paid to the natural world in OLOR ISCANUS than we might expect from this; the first poem, 'To the River Isca', depends far more upon rather dense literary allusion than upon natural observation. Nevertheless in it Vaughan implies his intention of remaining in his native place for the rest of his life.

> *When I am laid to* rest *hard by thy* streams,
>
> . . . .
>
> *I'll leave behind me such a* large, kind light,
> *As shall* redeem *thee from* oblivious night.

The promise has been amply kept, but it is SILEX SCINTILLANS rather than any other volume which is suffused with the atmosphere of the Usk Valley. It used to be said a few years ago, with dangerous half-truth, that *Vaughan's is the country of the mind,* as if he had not known and loved the natural world. One doubts if anyone could stay for even a few days in Scethrog or Talybont without realizing how deeply the sound of running water, the quality of light over the hills, and the rapid succession of sunshine, cloud and shower, had informed his imagination. So here, in one of the poems of literary compliment, 'Monsieur Gombauld', a passage that stands out is a home-made epic simile:

just so have I known
Some crystal *spring, that from the neighbour down*
Derived her birth, in gentle murmurs steal
To their next vale, and proudly there reveal
Her streams in louder accents, adding still
More noise and waters to her channel, till
At last swol'n with increase she glides along
The lawns and meadows in a wanton throng
Of frothy billows, and in one great name
Swallows the tributary brooks' drowned fame.

On the whole, though, in OLOR ISCANUS the natural world enters into Vaughan's verse by way of literary allusion, as in the first six lines of 'To my worthy friend Master T. Lewes', where the description of the snow-covered countryside and the frozen rivers is based upon a passage from Horace (ODES I, 9, lines 1–4); or in the elegy for 'Mr. R.W.', where the long description of the storm-ravaged trees is based upon the conflation of two passages in Virgil (AENEID IX, 697–82 and II, 626–31).

'To His Retired Friend, an Invitation to Brecknock', betrays Vaughan's patrician attitudes. He writes with equal contempt of the pulling down of the city's walls, so that it could not be used as a garrison town by either side in the Civil War, and of the commercial spirit of Brecon's inhabitants, clearly connecting their money-making propensities with their low desire to avoid what for Vaughan was a righteous conflict:

Thou'ldst swear (like Rome) *her foul, polluted walls*
Were sacked by Brennus, *and the savage* Gauls.
Abominable face of things! here's noise
Of banged mortars, blue aprons, and boys,
Pigs, dogs, and drums, with the hoarse hellish notes
Of politicly-deaf usurers' throats.

Marilla thought that the word 'mortars' in this passage referred to the piece of ordnance; this is unlikely, given the non-military character of the Brecon people at the time, and the immediate context, which is commercial (blue aprons are tradesmen; see OED blue *a* 13, and boys are probably servants; see OED boy sb^1 3). More likely is OED mortar sb^1 1d: 'applied to various mechanical appliances in which materials are pounded'. By 'politicly-deaf' Vaughan doubtless meant that the usurers pretended not to hear the requests of those who wanted to borrow money, in order to induce a sense of desperation in their clients, rather as antique-dealers will sometimes try to enhance the desirability of an object by pretending that it is not for sale. Here again, as in 'A Rhapsody', Vaughan reveals his capacity to evoke the excitement of a crowded urban scene. That he ceased altogether to write in this way may not be a great loss, set against the great (and in my view still largely undervalued) poetry of SILEX SCINTILLANS; nevertheless, those who love the poetry enough to want to know the man, will find such passages refreshing and revealing, even though a trace of anti-democratic feeling has to be admitted!

The author of the address to the reader prefaced to THALIA REDIVIVA (probably John Williams, who was prebendary of St. David's in 1678) describes Vaughan as known to be *very well able to give himself a lasting monument, by undertaking any argument of note in the whole circle of learning*. Whereas in SILEX SCINTILLANS Herbert and the Bible account for the vast majority of borrowings, in the secular poems, equally dense in allusion, the *range* of allusion is very much wider, making them both problematical and fascinating to the editor called upon to annotate them. Vaughan was doubtless still close enough to his formal education to enjoy writing in-group poems for his friends, and he moves easily between indigenous proverbs and classical learning, as in 'To his Retired Friend, an Invitation to Brecknock':

> *Or is the* palfrey *sick, and his rough hide*
> *With the penance of* one spur *mortified?*
> *Or taught by thee (like* Pythagoras's ox)
> *Is than his master grown more* orthodox?

Here the first allusion is to the proverb 'A spur in the head is worth two in the heel' (Tilley, PROVERBS IN ENGLAND, S791), meaning that a man rides hard when he is drunk; while the second depends for its interpretation (which I think earlier commentators have unnecessarily complicated) on the LIFE OF PYTHAGORAS by Iamblichus. A similar allusiveness is unremittingly at work in 'Upon a Cloak lent him by Mr. J. Ridsley', as well as an attractive sense of humour to which Vaughan did not often give expression. This poem, with its reference to *that day, when we/Left craggy Beeston, and the fatal Dee,* constitutes one piece of evidence that Vaughan was for a while engaged in active military service. With its affectionate ragging of Ridsley (who has never been identified), it also speaks for the quality of Vaughan's capacity for friendship; it suggests very well the kind of intimacy which is fostered by the shared hardships of military service. I find it one of the most engaging of the secular poems, but it would be hard to show why without quoting at length, since its point largely lies in the copiousness and fantasticality of invention, operating through varied allusion, by which the ridiculousness of the garment is thoroughly exploited. This poem is very much what Wordsworth was to call *a poem of the Fancy*.

Probably Vaughan's most important friend was Thomas Powell, rector of Cantref. It was probably Powell who steered OLOR ISCANUS through the press, and who had a hand in the skilfully written disclaimer of Vaughan's responsibility in the prefatory 'The Publisher to the Reader'. Powell contributed an interesting commendatory poem to OLOR ISCANUS, 'Upon the Most Ingenious Pair of Twins, Eugenius Philalethes, and the Author of these Poems'. He also contributed the verses on Vaughan as a poet of war, already mentioned, which were not printed until the publication of THALIA REDIVIVA in 1678. There is in OLOR ISCANUS a commendatory poem 'To my Learned Friend, Mr. T. Powell, Upon His Translation of Malvezzi's Christian Politician'; there is also a Latin poem praising Powell for his treatise on the elements of optics. Vaughan addressed to Powell two poems in THALIA REDIVIVA which are of biographical interest if, as one may suspect, they draw upon interests shared by the two men. L. C. Martin showed long ago that 'The Importunate Fortune, written to Dr. Powell of Cantref', draws, from lines 55–72, upon a passage in the hermetic books. More recently the other, 'To his Learned Friend and Loyal Fellow-Prisoner, Thomas Powell of Cantref, Doctor of Divinity', has been interestingly treated by A. U. Chapman in 'Henry Vaughan and Magnetic Philosophy', SOUTHERN REVIEW (University of Adelaide), Vol. IV, No. 3, 1971. E. L. Marilla, in his edition of Vaughan's secular poems, found this poem 'intensely obscure' and devoted an appendix to it as well as heavy annotation.

It will be clear from what follows that I disagree with Marilla's account of 'To his Learned Friend', but one does appreciate that it might seem 'obscure' in comparison with much of Vaughan's other work. Certainly it demonstrates abilities of a kind Vaughan did not often draw upon in SILEX SCINTILLANS. In the closeness and sequaciousness (and at times speciousness) of its logical progression it is as metaphysical as Donne in, say, 'Air and Angels'. It is Donnean too in the use it makes of 'scientific' knowledge (Vaughan draws brilliantly upon Gilbert's work on magnetism). Vaughan's use of the semantic history of certain words, simultaneously using both their Latin and their modern English meanings, is similar to the way Milton employs key words in PARADISE LOST. Indeed there is an academic obsessionalism about the way Vaughan deploys the *accuracy* of his linguistic knowledge in this poem that reminds one of George Herbert's deftness in the meaningful pun, or of Simon Gray's nice play on the word 'succinct' in 'Butley'. In order to demonstrate these qualities, it will be necessary to deal with the poem in some detail:

> *If severed friends by* sympathy *can join,*
> *And absent* kings *be honoured in their coin;*
> *May they do both, who are so curbed! but we*
> *Whom no such* abstracts *torture, that can see*
> *And pay each other a full self-return,*
> *May laugh, though all such* metaphysics *burn.*

Edmund Blunden noted that Vaughan's italics are often meaningful and so it seems here. 'Sympathy' (literally 'suffering together') probably has the meaning set out in OED Sympathy *sb*[1]: 'an affinity . . . by which (certain things) attract or tend towards each other'. The concept is employed at this point in a coolly intellectual way such as we associate with Donne rather than with Vaughan. Marilla's reference, in glossing these lines, to Thomas Vaughan's conception of the universal magnetic force suggests resonances which are here inappropriate. The second line too has an apparent Donnean coolness, reminding us of the reference in 'The Canonization' to 'the king's real, or his stampèd face'; but the context suggested by the title, and a likely date in the early 1650s, must remind us of ways in which kings may be absent: they may have been beheaded outside the Banqueting House, or they may be living in exile on the Continent. With this in mind, the line seems to contain a bitter joke upon those who prospered by collaborating with the King's enemies. Certainly these opening lines of the poem suggest the in-joking appropriate to a poem written to a close friend; they form a compliment by assuming Powell's easy response to the joke. Consider, for example, *we/Whom no such* abstracts *torture.* It may mean that the abstractions or abstruse ideas employed in the first two lines do not torture Vaughan and Powell: they are both intelligent men. It may mean (what the continuation suggests) that they are neither 'severed' nor 'absent', that they are not, to recall the Latin source of 'abstract', drawn away from each other (perhaps they are in the same prison). 'Abstracts' is a fairly abstract word, but its collocation with 'torture' suggests that Vaughan is seeing it in a comically concrete way, since the collocation suggests being 'pulled apart' by the rack. Henry and Thomas Vaughan both had a nice linguistic sense; apparently their teacher Matthew Herbert knew what he was about. The section ends with a similar piece of word-play. 'Metaphysics' in the popular sense of 'what is supernatural' cannot burn (though many books about metaphysics have been burned). The poem continues:

> *'Tis a kind soul in* magnets, *that atones*
> *Such two hard things as* iron *are and* stones,
> *And in their dumb* compliance *we learn more*
> *Of love, than ever books could speak before.*
> *For though* attraction *hath got all the name,*
> *As if that* power *but from one side came,*
> *Which both unites; yet, where there is no* sense,
> *There is no* passion, *nor* intelligence:
> *And so by consequence we cannot state*
> *A commerce, unless both we animate.*
> *For senseless things, though ne'er so called upon,*
> *Are deaf, and feel no invitation;*
> *But such as at the last day shall be shed*
> *By the great Lord of Life into the dead.*

This passage may be summarized in some such words as 'Friendship is not a one-sided matter'. Why then the extraordinarily tight and intricate argument? E. L. Marilla suggests that *the labored obscurity of the verses is sufficient indication that the author is studiously guarding himself against the public eye* and that *this sympathetic discourse of one Royalist to another was occasioned by some encounter of the latter with the Parliamentarian authorities.* This would seem to imply that if we could unravel the lines fully, we should come upon a political meaning which Vaughan would have been unwise to express more clearly. Marilla is, I think, misled by his belief that *In logic, there must have been some specific reason* for the re-assurances of *the author's friendship* contained in the poem. Why should there have been, given the existence of a tradition in which poets write, to friends, of their friendship? I would suggest rather that the lines are difficult (tightly argued, allusive) for the same reason (as they are in the same way) as many of Donne's are, that is, because they were written within an intellectual milieu in which the author wanted to keep his end up. Vaughan was a thorough-going intellectual; he was younger than Powell, whom he greatly admired; he doubtless wanted to impress him a bit. Marilla's suggestion that underlying these lines is the *Neo-Platonic idea that the Divine Spirit animates all things* is not so much inaccurate as inadequate to the specificity of the allusions. The point seems rather to be that the Elizabethan scientist William Gilbert, in his DE MAGNETE, had interpreted the old idea of an *Anima Mundi* in terms of magnetism: *The lodestone behaves . . . as if it were filled with life. Moreover, this is one and the same phenomenon which the ancients thought of as the soul in the heavens* (Chapman's translation, *art. cit.*, p. 226, note 29). Vaughan's lines are specific in their allusion in that the basic statement *Friendship is not a one-sided matter* is mediated through references to Gilbert's argument, which conveys a theory of magnetism different from that which had earlier prevailed, so that now, in contemplating the phenomena of magnetism, *we learn more/Of love, than ever books could speak before*—a fairly large claim, given that Vaughan must have been aware of the cosmic significance of love in Ficinian Platonism. Part of the wit of the passage lies in arguing from Gilbert's findings to a conclusion (such rare doctrine as gives *iron* life) which goes beyond Gilbert's reference to the lodestone behaving *as if it were filled with life.* Lines 11–16 contain five italicised words, all having some technical force. *Attraction* and *power* are best glossed by a passage from Gilbert: *The term 'attraction' has erroneously crept into magnetic philosophy from the ignorance of the ancients. Indeed, where there is attraction we see extraneous force, and a controlling power holds sway* (Chapman, *art. cit.*, p. 226, note 26). Against the idea that the phenomena of magnetism are to be explained in terms of 'extraneous force' and the sway of a 'controlling power' Gilbert puts forward the theory that magnetism represents an *agreeing together of both parts: the attractive power . . . residing not in one only but in both* (Chapman, *art. cit.*, p. 226, note 25). Gilbert suggested that the word 'coition' be substituted for 'attraction'. The word would have sat uneasily in Vaughan's poem, and the 'agreement' which Gilbert labelled 'coition' is here 'compliance' (line 9). In lines 11–14 Vaughan begins by referring to Gilbert's argument; but instead of continuing with something such as 'But it is rather the case that the phenomena of magnetism depend upon and exhibit mutuality and agreement rather than one-sided power' (which would only involve *metaphors* based upon vitalistic concepts), he instead plays with Gilbert's observation that the lodestone *behaves, indeed, as if it were filled with life,* and argues, in effect, that if there were no life there would be no magnetic phenomena. 'Sense' must be interpreted in terms of its common meaning 'faculty of sensation or perception' (OED Sense *sb*[1]) which is a technical term inasmuch as (and this Vaughan clearly implies) the faculty can only exist where there is soul: no sense without soul, no soul without life, therefore iron has life, is the way the argument goes.

Marilla glossed *passion* as 'emotional feeling' and *intelligence* as 'cognizance'. If for these we substitute OED Passion *sb*[5]: 'the fact or condition of being acted upon or affected by external agency' and OED Intelligence *sb*[5]: 'Communication, intercourse' (what Vaughan in other poems, as in line 16 here, calls 'commerce') it is not too difficult to see what is going on. Lines 11–16 are not too difficult either, though somewhat elliptical: The consequence of the foregoing argument is that we cannot declare the existence of a commerce ('agreement', 'compliance', etc.) unless we are prepared to attribute to the participants in that commerce soul and life; but the commerce between the iron and the lodestone is obvious enough, therefore . . . The argument is then reinforced by a further consideration, which merely relies upon the obvious meaning of 'senseless': (lines 17–20). The descent into platitude of the last four lines quoted should not be seen as one of Vaughan's failures to keep a poem going. It has, rather, the effect of relaxing the reader's awareness after the fair degree of intellectual tension induced by lines 7–16, so that the next lines carry the greater punch:

> *'Tis then no* heresy *to end the strife*
> *With such rare doctrine as gives* iron *life.*

This carrying of an apparently logical argument to an absurd conclusion is really very Donnean. Marilla comments that *Although this is obviously intended to appear whimsical, it is actually quite consistent with the previous argument.* Quite so, and one imagines that Powell would have seen the connection between the consistency and the whimsicality.

The poem continues, rather boringly:

> *For were it otherwise (which cannot be,*
> *And do thou judge my bold philosophy:)*
> *Then it would follow that if I were dead,*
> *Thy love, as now in life, would in that bed*
> *Of earth and darkness warm me, and dispense,*
> *Effectual informing influence.*

These lines don't, it seems to me, add very much to the poem. They are poignant inasmuch as they carry over into an inappropriate context thoughts which had haunted Vaughan when he was lamenting his dead brother William (see the first section of 'Sure, there's a tie of bodies' in the first part of SILEX SCINTILLANS). The fact that Vaughan can bring these thoughts into a rather playful context here suggests a date some time after the elegy.

Lines 29–32 begin the 'application':

> *Since then 'tis clear, that friendship is nought else*
> *But a joint, kind propension: and excess*
> *In none, but such whose equal easy hearts*
> *Comply and meet both in their* whole *and* parts.

Marilla wrote of this passage: *The syntactical snarl is, I believe, deliberate. The lines actually summarize the previous argument . . . the author would naturally feel compelled to keep the concept obscured.* This is interesting as the sort of error which can arise from erroneous assumptions—in this case that the poem is deliberately obscure because hiding a politically dangerous message. In sorting the passage out, one has to locate the source of the mental fog it induces—what Marilla called its 'syntactical snarl'. In my own attempt to do this, I hit upon 'excess' as the source of the difficulty, and just after doing so re-read the passage in the original edition, in which the penultimate [s] of 'excess' is long, that is, it looks somewhat like a manuscript [l]. If we substitute 'excels' for 'excess', we have a rhyme, not unimportant in a rhyming poem; not a very good rhyme in modern standard English, but Vaughan frequently rhymes [s] with [z] sounds; and we also have sense, a perfectly clear application of the train of thought concerning magnetism. The rest of the poem may be given without interruption:

> *And when they cannot meet, do not forget*
> *To mingle souls, but secretly reflect*
> *And some third place their centre make, where they*
> *Silently mix, and make an unseen stay:*
> *Let me not say (though* poets *may be bold,)*

Thou art more hard than steel, *than* stones *more cold,*
But as the mary-gold *in feasts of dew*
And early sun-beams, though but thin and few
Unfolds its self, then from the earth's cold breast
Heaves gently, and salutes the hopeful east:
So from thy quiet cell, *the retired throne*
Of thy fair thoughts, which silently bemoan
Our sad distractions, come: and richly dressed
With reverend mirth and manners, check the rest
Of loose, loathed men! why should I longer be
Racked 'twixt two evils? I see and cannot see.

Lines 33–36 continue in the same strongly metaphysical manner that has distinguished most of the poem to this point. As Marilla says, they form an assertion that the souls of friends can *unite at some projected point quite removed from their respective bodies.* Thomas Vaughan is relevant, remarking that *the soul can . . . infuse and communicate her thoughts to the absent, be the distance never so great* (ANTHROPOSOPHIA THEOMAGICA, p. 47). This gives the general idea but does not account for the idea in the poem of 'some third place'. The key is probably in whatever technical meaning may be assigned to 'secretly reflect'. It may be that the form into which Vaughan casts the idea is a compliment to Powell as the author of ELEMENTA OPTICAE; but to say this is some way from offering a precise explanation. The same consideration is relevant to the concluding words: *I see and cannot see.* This is ambiguous, as L. C. Martin notes: *I see you with my mind's eye (which is not enough) and cannot see you physically; or, I see much that I dislike seeing and do not see you.* The phrase 'two evils' suggests the second of these possibilities, a consideration which reinforces the likelihood that the poem was written when Powell's and Vaughan's political enemies were being especially troublesome. This *is*, surely, one of the meanings intended; if there is a more recondite meaning I have not discovered it. One gathers that pregnancy of statement is a virtue sought after in Welsh poetry; this might explain the extreme compression of these final lines.

What I like about the end of the poem is the way in which a different kind of 'magnetism' is used to modulate from tough intellectuality to a note of tenderness, a modulation for which the reader is psychologically prepared by *Let me not say . . . Thou art more hard than steel* and so on. The image of the *mary-gold* conveys more than simple tenderness, a fact we may overlook in the satisfaction of noting Vaughan's return to a more usual manner. That is, it is not merely what Thomas Vaughan would have called one of *a pack of small conspiracies*, not merely about the 'commerce' between the flower and the sun; it is about the way in which life renews itself in spite of the thinness and fewness of the sunbeams and the coldness of the earth; about renewal, about potentiality, in short about hope. That we are almost immediately brought up against 'sad distractions', 'loose, loathed men', and 'evils' does not extinguish the hope. It does lend it poignancy, and it gives added force to the already forcefully placed invitation 'come'—and it gives to the enigmatic last five words of the poem a quality of lament.

The exclusion of this poem and (for example) a politicly-edited version of Vaughan's elegy on

Charles Walbeoffe from the 1655 SILEX, suggests that Vaughan recognized the aesthetic weakness of POEMS 1646 and OLOR ISCANUS. It is not just a matter of religious feeling, but of artistic tact, that poems which are themselves good should be refused a place. They would have tended to fragment SILEX, which as it stands is a unity, into a collection of occasional poems. The evidence would seem to suggest that Vaughan, from time to time at all events, continued to write secular poems while he was engaged in the preparation of SILEX SCINTILLANS. He simply saw no reason to publish them. Their eventual publication in THALIA REDIVIVA may have owed more to the need to bulk out a memorial volume of his brother Thomas's work, than to re-emergence of literary ambition on Vaughan's part. One is glad to have them; but glad also of the integrity of SILEX.

Silex Scintillans

Hutchinson amusingly records that Whittier, writing during the American Civil War, censured *careless Vaughan* for bemocking his times; and that Courthope found in the tone of his poems the *epicurean indifference* of a *mere spectator* of his age's troubles, found indeed the marks of *a bad citizen*. Coarse as such criticisms are, they are not total misperceptions but, rather, grasp the wrong end of the stick. SILEX SCINTILLANS is among other things an attempt to live with, to accommodate to, to make creative use of, a barely tolerable pain: in Pauline terms a baptism into Christ's death in order to be baptised into His resurrection. The pain was that of private and public grief, intermingled and running together; his enemies, he said, *have washed their hands in the blood of my friends, my dearest and nearest relatives* (LIFE, 97). So thoroughgoing is the attempt that SILEX SCINTILLANS stands not merely as the monument to an individual life but as the record of, so to say, a geological shift in religious consciousness, interesting beyond the context of its own time, as students of Wordsworth and Coleridge will testify. The necessary condition of that attempt was detachment; and one might suggest that from the very beginning of his literary career the tension between detachment and involvement is important to Vaughan and to our attempt to understand him.

A suitable epigraph for SILEX SCINTILLANS might have been the Psalmist's *The sacrifices of God are a broken spirit: a broken and a contrite heart, o God, thou wilt not despise.* Vaughan expressed an essentially similar idea in the poem and its accompanying emblem which prefaced the 1650 edition of SILEX. The engraved title page shows a heart-shaped flint at which an arm, holding a conventional thunderbolt, is striking. Teardrops and flames are struck from the flint (see lines 11 to 12 of the poem). Three human faces are appearing under the blows and as Louis Martz noted *A man within can be clearly seen through an opening in the heart's wall.* L. C. Martin elucidates the emblem with a quotation: *Certain divine rays break out of the soul in adversity, like sparks of fire out of the afflicted flint* ('Flores solitudinis: of Temperance and Patience', p. 249). The burden of the poem which accompanies the emblem is that God has attempted unsuccessfully many times to capture Vaughan, and that Vaughan's obduracy has caused God to attempt another method, that of overcoming force with force. Vaughan interprets the troubles which have come upon him, the death of his younger brother and so on, as actions whereby God intends to bring about his conversion.

The penitential theme of the emblem and its accompanying poem are continued through two poems which may be regarded as prefatory matter, 'The Dedication' (the first stanza of which only appeared in the 1650 SILEX) and the pilcrowed poem 'Vain wits and eyes', and these repetitions of the penitential theme may be seen as deliberately establishing the context for the first major poem of SILEX I, 'Regeneration'. This poem may be profitably read in conjunction with Herbert's 'The Pilgrimage', from which it obviously derives; but whereas Herbert's poem has the simplicity of Bunyan's PILGRIM'S PROGRESS,

Vaughan's is a highly sophisticated and somewhat enigmatic entrance to his work. As its title implies, 'Regeneration' is a somewhat oblique record of that deepening of Vaughan's religious imagination which critics frequently refer to as his conversion-experience. Reading 'Regeneration' in this way, one can see why it had to be a more complex and a more obscure poem than Herbert's 'Pilgrimage'. The 'I' of that poem may be interpreted as Everyman or as Christian; the 'I' of Vaughan's poem is a good deal more difficult to generalize, even though the ground over which the 'I' passes is well documented in the literature of religious mysticism. A centrally important difference between Vaughan's situation and that of Herbert is that the elder poet was writing in a period of comparative religious and political tranquillity, when the Church of England was secure, whereas Vaughan is writing in a time of political trouble, when his church was in abeyance. One might say that a man of Vaughan's upbringing, living in South Wales at that time, had to create his own religious frame of reference if he was to have, and continue to have, a significant spiritual life. This poem has been interpreted with some plausibility as the record of the way in which Vaughan transferred his sense of the numinous from the church building itself (which had provided the titles and the starting points of so many of Herbert's poems), to the natural world, so that the 'grove' of stanza 5 with its 'stately height' and its branches which *met/And mixed on every side,* may be seen as a Bethel, a meeting place, within the natural world, between God and man; certainly in many poems Vaughan's imagination plays upon those meetings which recur through the earlier books of The Old Testament, in the days before the building of the Temple.

Structurally, 'Regeneration' may be seen as held together both by narrative sequence (the movement of the protagonist through the symbolic landscape) and by imagistic development (the way in which the frost, the surly winds, and the clouds of stanza 1 become transformed in the new spring which is announced in stanza 5 and beautifully described in stanza 6):

The unthrift Sun shot vital gold
A thousand pieces,
And heaven its azure did unfold
Chequered with snowy fleeces,
The air was all in spice
And every bush
A garland wore; thus fed my eyes
But all the ear lay hush.

I have argued elsewhere for the importance, to our understanding of this poem, of this imagistic development, whereby the natural appearances which are observed by the 'I' of the poem are transformed. This is contrary to the view that, in this poem and in others, Vaughan's natural references are to be interpreted as mere allegory *(Vaughan's is the country of the mind)*. It seems to me that the natural world is a presence within his work which goes beyond providing Vaughan correlatives for aspects of religious experience, and that, whereas most religious poets of his period merely wrote about mysticism, Vaughan was genuinely a nature-mystic, that is, he apprehended God in Nature. As his brother Thomas wrote *To speak of God without nature is more than we can do, for we have not known Him so.* It would seem, from the accounts quoted in William James' VARIETIES OF RELIGIOUS EXPERIENCE, that a greatly enhanced sense of the beauty and wonder of the natural world frequently accompanies the experience of religious conversion, as it does the experience of falling in love. I believe that such a heightened awareness of nature is an important element in 'Regeneration', that is, I believe that Vaughan is speaking directly from his own conversion-experience and not merely constructing allegories of religious events which he had read about in books. Vaughan was not alone in his own time in having a religious experience within which a sense of powerful insight into nature was an important component: Jacob Behmen the Silesian mystic had had such an experience, so profound and so far-reaching that he was convinced that he had understood the way in which God had, as it were, unfolded himself in the creation of the world. Closer to home, George Fox, the founder of the Society of Friends or Quakers, recorded an experience of insight into nature so intense that for some time he pondered within himself whether he ought not to become a physician, in order to employ for the good of mankind the knowledge of the physical world he had gained in that experience. Had Vaughan needed it, he might have found in Jacob Behmen a theological rationalization of his experience; for Behmen wrote that at the Fall, paradise had not been destroyed, but had merely, so to say, withdrawn behind the appearances of the natural world which we perceive in our everyday consciousness. This withdrawn, secret or hidden paradise, Behmen believed, is still available to the senses of the regenerate man, that is, the man who is reborn in Christ. Or, as Blake was to put it later, *If the doors of perception were cleansed everything would appear to man as it is, infinite.* Behmen's explanation of the transformed experiences which are available to the regenerate man suits very well the sense of nature which we find in a great many poems of Vaughan's; it is an awareness more dynamic, welling up from greater existential depths, than any mere allegorizing of religious meanings; and for us to apprehend the intensity and dynamism of Vaughan's communion with nature is partly to understand how it is that, in spite of there being no evidence that Wordsworth had read Vaughan's poems, critics are still wont to write of a possible relationship between them; for, surely, in both cases we are given a physical universe seen as unitary and as valuable, in contrast to the mechanistic universe, against which the Romantics were reacting, and which was gradually becoming the dominant mode of apprehending the physical world in Vaughan's time. This is not for one moment to deny the large and important differences between Vaughan's treatment of the natural world and that of the early romantics; but it might suggest why it was, that when Coleridge was engaged in the reading and thinking which underpinned the epistemological programme of romanticism, so much of that reading should have been among the poets and theologians of the early seventeenth century, including Jacob Behmen, to whom we have already referred. Limitations of space prevent an adequate reading of

'Regeneration' along the lines here suggested; the reader is referred to my essay 'Henry Vaughan and the Theme of Transfiguration' (SOUTHERN REVIEW, Adelaide, vol. I, 1963).

Though 'Regeneration' is a very strong and individual poem, one that memory is unlikely to confuse with any other poem of Vaughan's, it nevertheless exhibits a number of characteristics commonly found in his poems. Of these, some are 'metaphysical' in the sense that they appear to derive from the practice of Donne and of Herbert, for example, the dramatic way in which the poet as protagonist works through the poem. The importance within the poem of the personality of a particular individual author is something comparatively new in English religious verse, being hardly evident before Donne, whose method in so many poems was to dramatize his own religious conflicts. It has been quite justly observed that mediaeval religious verse is anonymous both in the sense that we usually do not know who the author was and also in the sense that who he was does not matter for our appreciation. By contrast Donne, Herbert and Vaughan project highly characteristic personalities into their poems. The opening of the poem, less dramatic perhaps than *Busy old fool, unruly sun* or *I struck the board, and cried, no more* is nevertheless arresting and shows the influence of the strong openings of Donne and of Herbert. Many of Vaughan's poems are virtually made up of tissues of Biblical allusions; this one is not; nevertheless, as the notes to my edition make clear, it is controlled by biblical allusion at important points. Another system of allusion within the poem, less obvious to the casual reader, links it with an especially interesting work of Henry Vaughan's brother Thomas, LUMEN DE LUMINE, and through that work with a number of Renaissance occultist authors. There is not space here to deal with those allusions, but I think it worth saying that, in my view, they support my interpretation of the poem as the record of a genuine mystical experience; again, see the essay cited above. Another characteristic, which recurs in a number of Vaughan's better poems, for example, 'The Waterfall', is the combination of accurate naturalistic observation with symbolic meaning. I am thinking here especially of the description of the stones in the fountain, some *bright and round/Others ill-shaped, and dull* which both corresponds with actuality (stones subjected to swiftly flowing water do become 'bright, and round') and also advances the meaning of the poem by the way in which the description carries both biblical and occultist allusions. Less characteristic, I think, though not unique in Vaughan's poems, is the emblematic quality of certain things in 'Regeneration', for example, the way in which the scales appear at the pinnacle of the mountain in the third stanza. Highly characteristic is the sense of spiritual activities within nature, which are understood by Vaughan in a strictly Christian frame of reference, though his perception of them may well be related to his reading in unorthodox writers.

Poems of Mourning

SILEX SCINTILLANS contains a number of elegies, which are marked by a pilcrow, or paragraph mark. These signs had been common in mediaeval manuscripts, were retained by the early printers and may be found in the Bible of 1611. It may be that their use in the Bible prompted Vaughan to use them here; he probably thought of the poems so marked as being especially holy because of the sacredness of his brother's memory. At all events, as a visual symbol the pilcrow links the elegies together in a way titles might not have done.

The first of these poems is 'Thou that know'st for whom I mourn'. This poem, with its simple rhyme scheme (abab, cdcd, etc.) and its long and short lines (octosyllabics alternating with trimeters) gives an effect of grief severely controlled, tightly held in. It may be that guilt is almost universally a component of grief; but there is something very typical of the seventeenth-century religious sensibility in the way in which Vaughan refers the death of his brother to his own sin (*But 'twas my sin that forced thy hand/To cull this* prim-rose *out*). The notion that God would take one brother in order to call the other to repentance and amendment of life is one that must seem strange, and self-regarding, to modern man, but one does not have to read far in the literature of the seventeenth century to find many analogues to Vaughan's thought here. In the first, and perhaps the first-written of these elegies, we might expect grief to predominate over consolation, and the consolation of lines

53–4 certainly seems more conventional than personally felt (*Thus, Lord, I see my gain is great,/My loss but little to it*); yet there is, hidden within the poem and not especially memorably expressed, a theme which Vaughan will elsewhere develop at his most quintessential, that of the secrecy of spiritual processes:

Thus hast thou placed in man's outside
Death to the common eye,
That heaven within him might abide,
And close eternity.

As we shall see, the hiddenness of man's life in God is a *motif* that Vaughan makes peculiarly his own.

Like so many of Vaughan's poems, this one ends with a prayer, and as so often he takes his language from Revelation:

Then make my soul white as his own,
My faith as pure, and steady,
And deck me, Lord, with the same crown
Thou hast crowned him already!

In 'Thou that know'st for whom I mourn', as we have seen, Vaughan expresses the thought that heaven and eternity abide within man, although what we can see of each other (our bodies) is subject to death. In the next pilcrowed poem, 'Come, come, what do I here?', Vaughan expresses the related thought that what the tomb contains is not dead, but asleep. The thought may seem to be a Christian commonplace, but there is nothing commonplace in the way in which

Vaughan develops it in various contexts, and the place it held in his mind and in that of his brother Thomas may well be due to its popularity in hermetic-Christian contexts. In this poem, the thought is given force by the obvious sincerity with which Vaughan, in the second stanza, refers to his own death, which he thinks of as both imminent and desirable.

At first reading, one may wonder why the poem 'Midnight' is marked with a pilcrow, since it is not explicitly a poem of mourning. It may be that it was so marked because it expresses the state of mind into which Vaughan had been thrown by his brother's death; as we have seen, a sense of guilt and its accompanying penitence is one of the marks of these poems. In 'Thou that know'st for whom I mourn', we have seen the theme of life hidden within apparent death; in this poem the life or 'quickness' of nature is explicitly contrasted with the poverty of life felt by the poet and, I would say, implicitly linked with the life of the dead person mourned in the other elegies: the connection is made explicit in the pilcrowed poem which follows next but one, 'Joy of my life! while left me here', where the imagery of stars is assimilated to the dead. 'Midnight' may be seen as a typical poem of the period in its use of the microcosmic theory (that is, in the comparison between man and the greater world). The comparison is one which a number of other poets had used; commonly, however, it is the steadfastness of the cosmos which is contrasted with the instability of man. Vaughan does, as in the poem 'Man', use that theme too; but here, and perhaps more typically, it is the liveliness and vitality of the greater world which is contrasted with the lack of spiritual vitality within man, man's lack of 'bright quickness', 'active brightness'.

There is some doubt about whether 'Joy of my life! while left me here' commemorates Vaughan's brother William or his first wife (see LIFE p. 94). One is tempted to think that the pattern which this poem makes upon the page is significant (as that of 'The Morning-Watch' may be); at all events it may serve to remind us that Vaughan, as a disciple of Herbert, was interested in using a considerable variety of stanza forms. As Vaughan has elsewhere expressed the thought that the work of an evil-minded author continues to wreak destruction after his death, so here he expresses the commonplace that the lives of good men continue to work for good after their individual deaths. I suspect that, commonplace as the thought may be, it was personally felt by Vaughan, who seems to have experienced himself as a person of considerable and distressing instability. He may well have come to feel, in the thoughtful months that followed his bereavement, that the experience of loss had been a stabilizing influence upon his life. However that may be, the expression of the thought is raised above commonplace in the poem by being mediated through one of Vaughan's great image-patterns, that of darkness and light, which will later be woven into what is perhaps his masterpiece, 'The Night', in the second part of SILEX SCINTILLANS. One has a sense, as one reads this poem, of Vaughan brooding within his local landscape upon his loss and upon the meaning of those deaths for his own life, and seeing that landscape made meaningful, as it were, by a biblical light. Apart from the assertion *God's saints are shining lights* at the beginning of stanza 3, stanzas 2 and 3 of the poem might be taken as naturalistic description of the way in which stars impinge upon the consciousness of a benighted traveller through the Usk valley. The effect of this is to endow the transition to the fourth stanza, with its quite explicit biblical allusions, with sublimity:

They are (indeed,) our pillar-fires
Seen as we go,
They are that City's shining spires
We travel to.

Notice here how the memory of the dead is likened to the fires which led the Israelites safely through the desert, and then how, in a splendid climax, the dead are experienced not simply as lights along the way, but as the very substance of the heavenly Jerusalem itself *(They are that City's shining spires);* this last seems to me to be a positively Blakean expression. The last four lines of the poem may well seem anti-climactic; I suspect that, for Vaughan himself, the thought of these lines was both of the greatest importance and neatly put. I understand that Welsh poetry went in for the epigrammatic: Vaughan may well have been pleased by the way in which the contrast between the words *out* and *in* encapsulate the whole Christian story from the Fall of Man to his ultimate salvation.

'Silence, and stealth of days' is rare among Vaughan poems in giving an indication of when it was written: *'tis now/Since thou art gone,/Twelve hundred hours;* twelve hundred hours is fifty days, and if we are to take this literally the poem may be dated in the first day or so of September 1648, since William Vaughan died about the 14th of July of that year. The thought of this poem rather resembles that of 'The Search', with William Vaughan in the role taken by Christ in that poem: Vaughan represents himself as attempting to recreate in imagination the sense of his brother still alive, as coming to realize the pointlessness of that attempt, and as thus arriving at a new sense of the vitality of the spirit: *souls must/Track one the other,/And now the spirit, not the dust/Must be thy brother.* We are reminded here of the great question *Can souls be tracked by any eye/But his, who gave them wings to fly?* ('Cock-Crowing'). These two quotations exemplify the way in which Vaughan, who like many fine poets was a great plagiarist, often transforms what he borrows. The thought of tracking souls seems to come from Habington's third elegy (to Talbot) *I cannot track the way, which thou didst go/In thy celestial journey.* Whether alluding to Habington or Owen Felltham, Vaughan was almost invariably able to improve upon his borrowing. There is some doubt about the reference to the *one pearl by whose light/All things I see* at the end of this poem. F. E. Hutchinson wrote that *The pearl may be his wife, or, as others think the Bible.* I think it unlikely that Vaughan would have described himself as seeing 'all things' by the light of any other human being, however beloved. The relevant background is surely Matthew xiii 45–6. That Vaughan should describe himself as finding heaven by the light of heaven is not really surprising.

In 'Sure, there's a tie of bodies!' we find Vaughan meditating on the fact that the emotions of the bereaved person gradually fade into the light of common day. The poem is more remarkable for the hermetic clothing which is given to the thought than for the thought itself, which may be reduced to the assertion that as Vaughan cannot keep with its first vividness the memory of the beloved person he has lost, he will substitute himself, as a *memento mori,* for the dead person. This is not the only occasion on which Vaughan dresses a basically simple idea in an expression which derives its complexity from hermeticism. For this aspect of the poem, the reader is referred to the notes of my edition.

The last of the pilcrowed poems in the first part of SILEX SCINTILLANS is 'I walked the other day'. Professor Louis Martz, in THE POETRY OF MEDITATION, calls it *the most explicit example of meditative structure to be found among the poems of Henry Vaughan.* Its nine stanzas may be seen as falling into three triads: in the first three stanzas Vaughan composes the image upon which his meditation is to focus; in stanzas 4 to 6 he seeks to understand the spiritual implications of that image; and in stanzas 7 to 9 the meditation turns to prayer, the 'colloquy with God' which was regarded as the proper end of meditation.

At the beginning of the poem it becomes clear that Vaughan is to record the experience of meditation:

I walked the other day (to spend my hour)
Into a field
Where I sometimes had seen the soil to yield
A gallant flower.

Here the phrase 'to spend my hour' almost certainly means that Vaughan's practice was to meditate regularly for an hour each day. When we know his work and that of his brother Thomas (who advised his readers that they should in the summer *translate themselves into the fields*) it seems natural that Vaughan should go 'into a field' to meditate. But Vaughan is not here being merely idiosyncratic; there was at the time he wrote a well established and flourishing tradition of meditation 'upon the creatures', and one of his favourite Old Testament characters had after all done the same thing: we read in Genesis xxiv 63 that *Isaac went out to meditate in the field at the eventide.*

The flower which is to be the focus of Vaughan's meditation is not to be seen because it is now winter: the poet therefore casts about for something with which to dig, and he finds the plant underground:

And by and by
I saw the warm recluse alone to lie
Where fresh and green
He lived of us unseen.

This image of a life hidden, humble, and flourishing is one of the most potent for Vaughan's imagination: it is used to convey both his sense of the spiritual state of his beloved dead, and his sense of himself as one who had completely given up the world in order to live a life *hidden with Christ in God.*

In Vaughan's understanding of the image, in the fourth stanza, there is nothing especially new, as he himself was perfectly aware (his intricate and rare questions were not answered). The understanding he arrives at is of course based upon St. Paul's discussion of death and resurrection in I Corinthians xv, but that is sufficient to lead him to the heart of his meditation, where it becomes clear that the hidden theme of the poem is his dead brother:

Happy are the dead!
What peace doth now
Rock him asleep below?

There is a good example here of the way in which Vaughan's poems assume biblical knowledge in their readers; here, for instance, we are expected to complete the quotation. The background is Revelation xiv 13 *Blessed are the dead which die in the Lord . . . that they may rest from their labours* (for readers who do not know Greek, it should be said that the word translated 'blessed' in the Authorized Version may equally be translated 'happy', as it is in The New English Bible). The point is that Vaughan is not making a general statement about the felicity of all dead people, or all dead creatures; his statement is to be understood as referring to the state of those who have 'died in the Lord'.

Having shined out in the very centre of Vaughan's meditation, the personal theme immediately recedes, and the sixth stanza of the poem is, so to say, a meditation on the process of meditation which the poem records; that is, Vaughan is thinking about the usefulness of meditation 'upon the creatures'.

In addressing God, in the seventh stanza of the poem, Vaughan singles out those of His attributes which are important for his present theme:

O thou! whose spirit did at first inflame
And warm the dead,
And by a sacred incubation fed
With life this frame
Which once had neither being, form, nor name.

Here there is an implicit argument: that is, the fact that God could create life out of dead matter, in the initial creation of the world, is guarantee that He can create life out of the dead matter of our individual bodies and bring us all to resurrection. As I have shown in writing of 'The Book', the argument implied is one that Vaughan may well have found in hermetic-Christian authors, though it may be equally well regarded as having biblical basis. Vaughan goes on to pray that he may so successfully track God in His creatures that he may eventually see the light of God himself and that (as he had seen the hidden life of the 'poor root') so he may again see the life of him *At whose dumb urn/Thus all the year I mourn.* A beautifully structured poem, and one in which Vaughan successfully blends the personal and the objective; anyone who has attempted some such form of Christian meditation must regard it as a highly successful meditation!

The Secrecy of Religious Growth and the 'Quickness' of Nature

The Christian religion has at its heart a kind of paradox; that of triumph built upon defeat, of eternal life rising from the death upon the cross; and one cannot read far either in the Bible or in Christian theology without coming to an awareness that Christian language tends to the paradoxical. In fact it has been analysed by some theologians as operating in an essentially similar way to the language of poetry. Related to what I have called the central paradox of Christianity is the paradoxical statement in Luke xvii 33: *Whosoever shall seek to save his life shall lose it; and whosoever shall lose his life shall preserve it.* Then there is the language of St. Paul in I Corinthians xv, which we have already noted. Central to the poem we have just been looking at is the image of the plant which appears to be dead but is really alive, which is in fact recovering from the period of its more apparent life *(Did there repair/ Such losses as befell him in this air).* The relevance to Vaughan's meditation on his dead brother is brought out in the following stanza in the words *Happy are the dead!* The image corresponds to a sense we have when reading Vaughan that real life is where the majority of people would be least likely to look for it. Stated in this abstract way, this might seem to be a Christian enough theme, and so in a sense it is; yet Vaughan's expression of this theme is unlike that of most other religious poets, and strikes one as springing from the depths of his sensibility rather than being merely the product of devotional reading. It is expressed in a number of characteristic images: the root hidden underground in the winter, the grave as a womb, the bed as a grave/womb. In connection with this particular cluster of images, in which death is seen to intensify into life, darkness into light, sleep into waking, Thomas Vaughan's definition of death is interesting. He wrote that death is *a recession of life into the hiddenness: not the annihilation of any one particle but a retreat of hidden natures to the same state they were in before they were manifested* (ANTHROPOSOPHIA THEOMAGICA). There is a similar sense of what death is in Vaughan's poem 'Resurrection and Immortality':

> *For no thing can to* Nothing *fall, but still*
> *Incorporates by skill,*
> *And then returns, and from the womb of things*
> *Such treasure brings*
> *As* Phoenix-*like renew'th*
> *Both life, and youth;*
> *For a preserving spirit doth still pass*
> *Untainted through this mass.*

We see from this that Vaughan views all existence as essentially cyclical; that the process of dying into life is brought about by the spirit of God working directly in the phenomena, and, one often feels when reading Vaughan, working most significantly when working secretly and upon that which is apparently dead. Mr. D. P. Norford of Dartmouth college, in an unpublished essay which he has kindly allowed me to see, has suggested that these images of Vaughan may be seen as representing the regenerative potential of the unconscious mind, and in fact the categories of Jungian psychology seem appropriate in thinking about this characteristic element in Vaughan's poetic output. The importance of the paradoxes and the image clusters I have mentioned may be suggested merely by considering Vaughan's great anthology-pieces: 'The Morning-Watch', 'The Night', 'Childhood' and so on. I want now to look at 'The Morning-Watch' in some detail.

In commenting on the phrase *to spend my hour* in the poem 'I walked the other day' I suggested that Vaughan was referring to a regular period of meditation. The title of 'The Morning-Watch' may well be related to Vaughan's practice in this matter. In Exodus xiv 24 we read that *It came to pass . . . in the morning watch* and a marginal note in a Bible printed in 1649 explains *about the three last hours of the night.* This would be from 3 to 6 o'clock, as the OXFORD ENGLISH DICTIONARY makes clear. It seems likely that Vaughan had in mind both this usage, and the sense of watching as a devotional exercise or religious observance (also documented in OED). Vaughan's devotional prose work, THE MOUNT OF OLIVES, begins with 'Admonitions for Morning Prayer' which contain a number of parallels to the phrasing and sense of this poem.

E. C. Pettet, who has written well on 'The Morning-Watch', remarks that on paper it may appear rather formal in its patterning of long and short lines. Any sense of formal stiffness that we may derive through the eye quickly gives way to a delighted recognition of the glorious lyrical impulse which energizes the poem. It may be, though, that the visual patterning of the poem is meaningful, in a way similar to that of George Herbert in such poems as 'Easter Wings'; I am thinking of the fact that the poem falls into nine sections (regarding each set of long lines and each set of short lines as a section) and that this is a significant number, given Vaughan's theme of the harmony of creation. There were nine orders of angels and nine planetary spheres.

As we have seen, it can be helpful when reading Vaughan to recognize when he is quoting or alluding, and this applies almost as much where the poems of George Herbert are concerned as it does to the Bible. The first line of 'The Morning-Watch' echoes the first line of Herbert's 'The Holy Scriptures' (1) which begins *Oh book! infinite sweetness!* E. C. Pettet suggests, and I think correctly, that Vaughan is using the phrase from Herbert's poem, and probably its context, for the implied assertion that the book of nature is truly comparable with the book of the scriptures for the divine lessons that it contains. The likelihood that Vaughan had that particular poem of Herbert's in mind when he wrote 'The Morning-Watch' is increased by the fact that line 23 of the poem, where the phrase *O let me climb* means *to pray,* is an echo of the meaning, though not of the exact phrasing, of the last line of Herbert's sonnet. Very often too, a knowledge of Vaughan's prose works will provide useful background and context to the poems. Here, for example, the words *This dew fell on my breast* (line 7) may be understood by reference to a passage in Vaughan's THE MOUNT OF OLIVES: *Sanctify and supple my heart with the dew of thy divine spirit:* it is obvious that what Vaughan has in mind is not naturalistic dew, but the operations of the third Person of the Holy Trinity. The section of the poem most likely to arouse immediate delight is from line 9 to line 18:

> *In what rings,*
> *And* hymning circulations *the quick world*
> *Awakes, and sings;*
> *The rising winds,*
> *And falling springs,*
> *Birds, beasts, all things*
> *Adore him in their kinds.*
> *Thus all is hurled*
> *In sacred* hymns, *and* order, *the great* chime
> *And* symphony *of nature.*

Here Vaughan evokes (one might almost say re-creates) the order and the vitality of nature, that order which was thought by some ancient theologians to reveal the operation of God the Father within the cosmos, and that vitality which was thought to arise from the operation of Christ the Son. In its celebration of order, this passage goes back to Plato's TIMAEUS, a dialogue on the creation of the world, in which it is argued that the heavenly bodies' circular motion, by which time is measured, gives us a moving image of eternity. The words '*rings,/And* hymning circulations' clearly refer to this Platonic and Pythagorean tradition: the idea that the circular motion of the heavenly bodies produces 'hymning' goes back to the Pythagorean idea that the mathematical intervals to be discerned among the planets are indicative of heavenly harmonies. (This idea, like others in this poem, may be explored in the annotations of any good edition of Milton's 'On The Morning of Christ's Nativity.') Vaughan does not, however, confine himself to the idea of the circularity, the regularity, of the heavenly bodies; of perhaps more interest to him, is the vitality and dynamism to be perceived within the cosmos: he writes of 'the *quick* world', using 'quick' in its old sense of 'living'. Vaughan's meaning here is nicely suggested by a quotation from his brother Thomas's ANTHROPOSOPHIA THEOMAGICA: *the world, which is God's building, is full of spirit, quick, and living.* It is very typical of Vaughan that in contemplating the book of the creatures he should not confine himself to such prestigious 'creatures' as the heavenly bodies; he is interested in all the rungs of the ladder of nature: birds, beasts, all things. As so often in Renaissance poetry, what at first glance might appear to be sheer spontaneous lyricism, turns out on closer inspection to be carefully structured. In this instance the quoted passage begins and ends with a similar idea, returning to the reference to circularity and the hymning of nature, so that the lines both display and allude to circularity. Here I would take issue with E. C. Pettet who sees Vaughan's use of the word 'hurled' in line 16 as a blemish on the poem; he calls it *rhyme-forced and inappropriate* in a context of *sacred hymns and order.* This is because Pettet sees the connotations of the word as being violent agitation and disorder. I think, to the contrary, that the word is perfectly chosen, because it incorporates both the sense of order and the sense of vitality and dynamism which I have been noticing; this is because of the association between the words 'whirl' and 'hurl' which are noticed in the OED entries for both words, and which Pettet has overlooked. That is, I think that we are to understand the *sense* 'whirled' as primary here, with its suggestion of rapid circular motion, while the *form* of the word suggests the dynamism and vitality of nature. The relevant meaning of the word 'chime' is *a system of which all the parts are in harmony, showing a correspondence of proportion and relation* (OED); and the word 'symphony' is to be understood in its Latin sense of concord and harmony. The appropriateness of the word is perhaps better understood if we recall that an Elizabethan could think of music as deriving from, as being in a sense an imitation of, the motion of the stars, the agreement of the planets, and the celestial circles. The sense of joy which this passage undoubtedly exhibits is theologically proper when we consider the implications of Vaughan's insistence upon the cosmic harmony; for the fact is that the cosmic harmony had been, according to orthodox Christian tradition, destroyed at the Fall of man, a fact which is given considerable space in Milton's PARADISE LOST. As Dixon suggests, *By hearing this symphony of nature Vaughan is actually entering into the consciousness of unfallen man.* This suggestion may at first glance seem startling, and theologically inappropriate, but it certainly helps to explain the sense of joy which the poem undoubtedly expresses. And we can find a sort of theological justification for the notion when we remember the words of a near contemporary of Vaughan, the Silesian mystic Jacob Behmen, who wrote that at the Fall Paradise was not destroyed, but was merely *swallowed up in the Mystery,* that is, within the world of revealed objects, and that *it is not altered in itself, it is only withdrawn from our view . . . for if our eyes were opened we should see it* ('Forty Questions Concerning the Soul'). Behmen also wrote that *the right man regenerate and born anew in Christ . . . is in the paradise of God.* That is, Behmen was arguing that that paradise which was enjoyed by Adam and Eve before the Fall is still there, as it were hidden beneath the phenomena available to our everyday perception, and may be enjoyed by the man who is 'born again'. If we take this idea as being possibly relevant to this particular poem of Vaughan's, as I am convinced it is to others, then we can see that what the poem is rejoicing in is the biblical experience of being born again of water and the spirit, words which are clearly relevant to the opening of the poem; that is, it is another treatment of the theme which Vaughan had already treated in 'Regeneration'. I should say here that I now believe my note on line 22 of the poem (*Whose* echo *is heaven's bliss*) is strained and almost certainly wrong. It now seems to me that the simpler interpretation is almost certainly the correct one: that is, that the bliss of heaven is available in the here and now to the man praying, as immediately and as certainly as an echo will follow speech when the physical circumstances are right; that is, heaven's bliss is what answers prayer, as the echo is what answers speech.

If we consider this poem as being importantly related in its central meaning to 'Regeneration', we may well note that one important difference between the two poems is that in the earlier the reader has a very strong sense of Vaughan as protagonist walking through the symbolic landscape, whereas here our sense of the person referred to in the beginning of the poem ('my soul') very soon fades as our consciousness becomes turned from Vaughan's little world to the macrocosm or 'greater world'. The transition in which the sense of 'I' fades out, is not altogether surprising if one has read fairly widely in the hermetic literature with which we know Vaughan was familiar. Whereas orthodox Christianity tended to stress a gulf between man and the rest of God's creation, hermetic Christians rather emphasized that man was part of nature, indeed their manner of viewing the relationship between man and the rest of creation in a sense looks forward to our twentieth century interests in ecology. The transition, it seems to me, is effected in the lines

> *This dew fell on my breast;*
> *O how it* bloods,
> *And* spirits *all my earth!*

Here, we see, the phrase 'my earth' may be understood as referring both to Vaughan's mortal flesh, and to the physical universe of which he is a part; the former meaning looks back over the preceding part of the poem, while the latter looks forward to the passage on the great world which immediately succeeds. There is a great deal more to be said about this poem; one would like to undertake an examination of the way Vaughan achieves its beautiful sound-effects, for example; but there is not space. Let me just mention that the ending of the poem, while its imagery is characteristic of Vaughan, may also derive from the ending of Shakespeare's complex and beautiful sonnet, 'That time of year thou may'st in me behold'.

One's guess that 'The Morning-Watch' arose from Vaughan's own meditative practice is strengthened by what he writes in his didactic poem 'Rules and Lessons'. In the second stanza, Vaughan advises readers *never sleep the sun up* and *Rise to prevent the sun.* That his morning prayer encompassed meditation on the creatures becomes clear from the third stanza:

> *Walk with thy fellow-creatures: note the* hush
> *And* whispers *amongst them. There's not a* spring,
> *Or* leaf *but hath his* morning-hymn; *each* bush
> *And* oak *doth know I AM.*

Here, in the phrase, 'morning-hymn', we see that as in 'The Morning-Watch' Vaughan understands the 'creatures' themselves to be praising God. Donne and Herbert had both considered this notion and rejected it in favour of the idea that it is man, as high-priest of the creation, who offers up praise to God on behalf of a universe which, being inarticulate, cannot offer its own praises. This acceptance of an animistic or vitalistic interpretation of things is typical of Vaughan. Typical also is his sense, in the reference to each bush and oak knowing I AM, that the natural world retains an enjoyment of close relationship with God as in the early days of mankind recorded in the Pentateuch, even though for man the close relationship no longer exists. Though there is evidence in his poems on both sides of the question, one feels that Vaughan's instinctive feeling was against the orthodox view that nature had become corrupted at the Fall of man. If, as has been suggested, Vaughan was especially attracted by early morning, there is a neatly-put clue to the reasons in 'Rules and Lessons':

> Mornings *are* mysteries; *the first world's* youth,
> *Man's* resurrection, *and the future's* bud
> *Shroud in their births.*

Vaughan is, I think, using the word mystery here in a sense not unlike its technical theological sense; he is seeing mornings as having a kind of sacramental significance, partially concealing and partially revealing certain spiritual truths. If one attempts to make a list of Vaughan's interests or themes as illustrated in the poems of SILEX SCINTILLANS, then the three concepts suggested in the above quotation must have a place: Vaughan's imagination was clearly moved by the early books of the Bible, in which he descried a world, after the Fall it is true, which nevertheless retained something of the prelapsarian ability to converse with God and with God's ambassadors. In 'Regeneration', and in 'The Morning-Watch', we have seen how the idea of man's regeneration appeals to his imagination: the regeneration which is new every morning, the regeneration which seizes upon a man's life and changes its tone and direction, and of course in other poems there is concern with the resurrection from the dead. More subtly, in a number of poems one can perceive what might be called a philosophy of potentiality ('the future's *bud*'), an element in Vaughan's work which, I have argued elsewhere, arises from his interest in hermetic philosophy and which, one might add, indicates in him affinities, not immediately apparent, with such later artists as William Blake and D. H. Lawrence. It is obvious in 'I walked the other day', for example, that what interests Vaughan about the 'poor root' is not what it is in its withdrawn winter existence, but what that withdrawnness and that hiddenness is preparing for; as may be seen in 'Resurrection and Immortality', Vaughan denies the reality of death itself.

It seems to me that Vaughan's philosophy of potentiality is related to another characteristic concern of his verse, that is, the dynamism of nature. This sense of the natural world being constantly in motion, constantly in a state of flux from one condition into another, is one that is very frequently expressed: see for example 'Rules and Lessons' lines 87 to 90:

> *here* fountains *flow,*
> Birds *sing,* beasts *feed,* fish *leap and the* earth *stands fast;*
> *Above are restless* motions, *running* lights,
> *Vast circling* azure, *giddy* clouds, *days, night.*

Or one may look at 'The Tempest' lines 25 to 28, in which the physical activity of nature is explicitly related to nature's spiritual aspirations:

> *All things here show him heaven;* waters *that fall*
> *Chide, and fly up;* mists *of corruptest foam*
> *Quit their first beds & mount; trees, herbs, flowers, all*
> *Strive upwards still, and point him the way home.*

Here of course 'him' is man, who is being asked to learn the lessons so lavishly given him in the natural world *(all the vast expense/In the Creation shed, and slaved to sense/Makes up but lectures for his eye, and ear.)*

Another good example of Vaughan's expression of natural dynamism comes in 'Affliction' (1):

Beauty consists in colours; and that's best
Which is not fixed, but flies, and flows;
The settled red *is dull, and* whites *that rest*
Something of sickness would disclose.
Vicissitude plays all the game,
Nothing that stirs,
Or hath a name,
But waits upon this wheel.

The common quality of the passages I have been quoting is one of movement, energy, *process;* this quality is characteristic of the verse of Silex Scintillans rather than of the earlier verse. It is obvious that verse such as this cannot be reconciled with the old critical tradition which says that a poem should be a 'speaking picture'. Vaughan has no special interest in the colour, texture, the shape or form of objects; indeed though many of his images are in a sense visual, their visual quality is not what we notice about them. What we do notice is a sense of energy, movement, change of state. As Helen O'Grady wrote *At the level of sensory images, Vaughan's emphasis is always on the activity, the dynamic quality of impressions. His vital world is constantly moving, changing, a kaleidoscope of light and shadow and dynamic forms.* This seems to me a most accurate and valuable description of the quality in Vaughan's verse that I have tried to isolate, of the sense we have that what Vaughan attended to was the general elusive impression of the passing moment, the dynamic harmony produced by constant flux.

This quality in Vaughan's poetry is related, one feels sure, to the fact of his living in the Usk Valley, with its shifting sunshine, cloud and shower and the incessant sound of running water; it is also related to his interest in the hermetic philosophy, which in this instance reinforced a sense of things that he must have absorbed unconsciously from earliest boyhood. In its 'scientific' aspect of alchemy, hermeticism is above all concerned with *process*. The essence of the alchemical operation is that the possibilities of matter are realized in turn in a process of transformation through the various grades of existence. In its more purely philosophical aspect, hermeticism accounts for the created world in terms of emanation and return to source, in terms, that is, of endless cyclic movement. In the hermetic books, there is frequent stress on the energy, the working that goes on in the cosmos. With the passage from 'Rules and Lessons' quoted above in mind, consider this passage:

God is not idle; if he were then all things would be idle; for all things are full of God. Nay, in the Kosmos also there is no idleness anywhere; idleness, whether of the maker or of that of which he makes, is a word devoid of meaning. It needs must be that all things come into being, and that things are coming into being always and everywhere. For the maker is in all things; his abode is not in some one place, nor does he make some one thing; no, he makes all things and everywhere he is at work.

Consider also this passage, in which Thomas Vaughan is translating Cornelius Agrippa:

But after the spirit has failed through the perishable courses amidst which it is dispersed, it is presently purged from all impurity, and changes into innumerable forms, here into herb and there into stone, or perchance into some extraordinary animal; but now and then into a cloud, a pearl, some gem or metal; and sweetly glittering with blushing flames, it passes continually through a myriad changes of colours, and lives always an operator and magus of prodigies, never wearying with the toil thereof but ever young in strength and energy.

Given Henry Vaughan's demonstrable immersion in hermetic ideas, expressed as they so often were in passages like the two just quoted, it is not surprising that Helen O'Grady should find in his poems *some alchemical transformation of images, that . . . raises a defensive wariness in the reader nurtured on twentieth century poetry and criticism.*

It seems to me that Helen O'Grady's formulation is accurate. Vaughan's most characteristic poems do express a sense of energy, of process, of interrelationship and communion between the eternal, celestial, and terrestrial worlds. Given his circumstances and his intellectual interests, one would expect his verse to conjure up a world (to use Thomas Vaughan's phrase) *full of spirit, quick and living,* rather than one made like the work of a carpenter *without any infusion of life.* I would suggest, indeed, that our pleasure in Vaughan's poetry lies in the apprehension in it of a world very different from the model which we still unconsciously retain from eighteenth-century mechanics. Vaughan's imagery betrays not so much an awareness of nature or of the realm beyond nature, as of a sphere beyond matter within the material world itself; and this too is what we would expect of a hermetic poet, for (in the words of Jacob Behmen which have already been quoted in connection with 'The Morning-Watch') *Paradise is in the world . . . swallowed up in the Mystery . . . but it is not altered in itself, it is only withdrawn from our view . . . for if our eyes were opened we should see it.*

What I have said of the influence of hermeticism upon Vaughan's sense of the dynamism of nature is not to suggest that Vaughan's outlook was wholly determined by hermetic philosophy; it seems to me rather that both his personality and the life-habit of his most creative years made him as it were intuitively a hermetist. The contribution of the hermetic philosophy to his poetry, it seems to me, was that it provided him with a coherent system of thought, and, further, with a terminology which helped him to actualize his religious intuition of a God-animated universe.

Meditations on the Life of Christ

Meditation on the life of Christ, an important element in Catholic spirituality from mediaeval times, remained influential in the seventeenth century, as Professor Martz makes clear in THE

POETRY OF MEDITATION. Although Vaughan could have described himself, like his brother Thomas, as a *true, resolute Protestant in the best sense of the Church of England* (ANTHROPOSOPHIA THEOMAGICA) he did not hesitate to make use of Catholic spiritual writings. A number of his poems may be described as meditations on the life of Christ, for example 'The Search', 'The Incarnation, and Passion', 'The Passion', 'Christ's Nativity' (SILEX I); and 'Ascension Day', 'Palm-Sunday', 'Jesus Weeping' (I and II), 'The Dwelling-Place', and 'The Night' (SILEX II).

Professor Martz suggests that an important difference between mediaeval and counter-Reformation Catholic teaching about meditation on the life of Christ was that the earlier period stressed the humanity of Christ and the later the paradox of God-made-man. In this respect Vaughan was of his time; see for example the section 'Admonitions, With Meditations and Prayers to be used before we come to the Lord's Supper' in his prose work, THE MOUNT OF OLIVES. He advises his readers that they should, on the day they are to partake of the Sacrament, after two days at least of self-examination and penitence,

be up with the day, or rather with the Saviour, who rose up early, while it was yet dark . . . Consider how he left his Father's bosom to be lodged in a manger, and laid by his robes of glory to take upon him the seed of Abraham . . . *When thou hast thus considered him in his acts of love and humility consider him again in his glory, take thine eyes from off* Bethlehem *and* Golgotha *and look up to the Mount of Olives, yea, to Heaven where he sits now upon the right hand of his Father, Angels, principalities and powers being made subject unto him.* (M 157–8).

The fact that Vaughan regarded such meditations as necessary in preparing for the Lord's Supper is worth remembering, as we read those of his poems which deal with the life of Christ.

The Catholic context, sketched above, which is dealt with fully in Martz's chapter 'Meditations on the Life of Christ' provides some essential background for an understanding of some of the poems listed above; but it seems to me that there is a more immediate context in Protestant and Anglican, and occasionally hermetic thought which is equally important. 'The Search' suggests such a consideration. For example, why does Vaughan, after spending some 70 lines recalling major episodes from the life of Christ, in the manner recommended in the manuals and in his own MOUNT OF OLIVES, apparently repudiate that method in the final, stanzaic section of the poem? Why is the poem, in other words (Stanley Fish's words, though he does not deal with Vaughan), a *self-consuming artifact,* why does it become the *vehicle of its own abandonment?* We perhaps come towards an answer if we recall that a central problem for doctrinal debate during the Reformation and counter-Reformation was the question of where, and by extension how, do we find Christ. The 'where' had been the subject of the first conversation between Jesus and his disciples recorded in St. John's gospel (i 38, 39): *They said unto him, Rabbi . . . where dwellest thou? He saith unto them, Come and see.* That Vaughan considered the implications of this exchange, in a manner which sheds some light upon 'The Search', is obvious from 'The Dwelling-Place' in SILEX II:

My dear, dear God! I do not know
What lodged thee then, nor where, nor how;
But I am sure, thou dost now come
Oft to a narrow, homely room,
Where thou too hast but the least part,
My God, I mean my sinful heart.

The question of where to find Jesus relates closely to the question of the Real Presence of Christ in the Sacrament. On the one hand is the Roman position, that at the consecration the bread and wine became the Body and Blood of Christ: on the other hand the Anglican Church regarded this doctrine of transubstantiation as *repugnant to the plain words of Scripture* and as having *given occasion to many superstitions* (Article 28, Book of Common Prayer). Opposition to the Roman doctrine in the Thirty-Nine Articles did not close off Anglican thinking, and the interested reader will find valuable discussions, from Hooker to James Ussher, in More and Cross's anthology ANGLICANISM (see the section 'The Eucharistic Presence'). Donne put forward the Anglican position in his splendid Easter-Day Sermon of 1630, taking as his text the words of the angel to the women seeking Christ at his sepulchre (Matthew xxviii, 6): *He is not here: for he is risen,* a key text in this debate: (THE SERMONS OF JOHN DONNE, ed. Simpson and Potter, Vol. IX, no. 8). Donne writes *Because he is risen, he cannot be here in the Sepulchre, so, as that you may embalm his body, Because he is ascended, he cannot be here, here in the Sacrament, so, as you may break or eat that body.*

Debate about the presence, or the mode of the presence, of Christ in the Sacrament focused philosophical differences. Reformation debate about desirable forms of worship also involved historical considerations, since it was felt important to discover and re-create the worship of the early Church. Historical discussion, like philosophical speculation, could become sterile when taken to extremes, and so we find Jacob Behmen inveighing against *titular, nominal or historical Christians* (see his First Epistle).

With this background in mind, we may imagine Vaughan, a member of the Church of England deprived of his customary religious observances after the defeat of the Royalists, trying to keep alight a spiritual flame for himself and others and asking where Christ may be found. In such circumstances, visualization of the life of Christ, as recommended in the manuals of meditation, would have an obvious usefulness; it would be natural for the *objective* tendencies in Catholicism to appeal. On the other hand, Vaughan would have been profoundly influenced by the *subjective* tendencies of Protestantism—and Anglicans of the seventeenth century certainly regarded themselves as Protestants. *The kingdom of God is within you* (Luke xvii 21) was a text of enormous importance; a Protestant mystic like Behmen placed great stress on the necessity of individual salvation, and saw the sacraments of the Church as ineffectual unless they were considered as symbols of inward regeneration. Vaughan's poems on the life of Christ show the interaction between the objective, Catholic approach and the subjective Protestant approach.

'The Search' indeed shows a clear progress from the objective to the subjective. The poem begins strikingly, and in the present tense:

'Tis now clear day: I see a Rose
Bud in the bright East, and disclose
The Pilgrim-Sun.

At this point in our reading, these lines may be taken as a rather literal description of the dawning day; when we return to them after experiencing the entire poem, we may well find symbolic resonances. The poet immediately turns to the past tense, which modulates into the historic present in line 21 when the framework of past tense is firmly established. The *material* of what follows is what we might expect to find recommended in the manuals when they are advocating meditation on the life of Christ. However the rapidity of Vaughan's account, with its frequent verbs, justifies the strong phrase 'roving ecstasy' of the fourth line; and that phrase itself shows us how a poet can transform, or make experiential, a technical term ('ecstasy' as used here is related to its use by mystical writers; it named the state of rapture in which the body became incapable of sensation, while the soul was engaged in the contemplation of divine things). Such verbs as 'I have been' and 'have seen' may be related to the recommendations of the devotional manuals, but give the poem a dramaticity which is Vaughan's own, and which relates him to the other metaphysical poets, and especially to Donne. Typical of Vaughan too is the way in which, from line 21, he takes us back to the still earlier time of the patriarchs, the chronicle of which he loved so well, as many poems attest. Students of Vaughan almost necessarily become students of the Bible, and they may not find this apparent digression unsuitable, since the New Testament makes it clear that Jesus himself had Scriptual scene and saying continually in his mind. In lines 15–20, the historical fact of the destruction of Jerusalem in AD 135, after the collapse of the bar-Kochba rebellion, gives Vaughan the opportunity to use a favourite image. He writes that he was shown

A little dust, and for the Town
A heap of ashes, where some said
A small bright sparkle was a bed,
Which would one day (beneath the pole),
Awake, and then refine the whole.

This is basically the same image of the remnant of an earlier fire, hidden by ashes but containing the potentiality for a new flame, which Vaughan used in the poem 'Rules and Lessons', lines 133–4, and the end of 'The Morning-Watch'. It is a favourite image, one suspects, because it embodies what was for Vaughan a profoundly important theme or *motif:* that of potentiality. Looked at in this way, it may be regarded as closely related to the apparently very different image of the 'poor root' of 'I walked the other day', except that in 'The Search' the potentiality of which Vaughan is speaking is, so to say, the primal potentiality in which all others participate, from which all others derive, for here of course the image refers to the Resurrected Christ and looks forward to the Second Coming. Donne, in the Easter-Day Sermon already referred to in this section, reminds his hearers that the Resurrection of Christ is not the only raising from the dead narrated in the Bible, but that all others are referred to in the passive voice (*Suscitatus* in the Vulgate), whereas the Resurrection of Christ is referred to here in the active voice *(Surrexit)*. It is because of this primacy of Christ's potentiality that St. Paul, in the biblical verse appended to this poem, is able to say that *in Him we live, and move, and have our being.*

The reader will notice that the chronological scheme (following the course of Christ's life on earth) is broken at the point where the poet decides *I'll to the wilderness;* Martz explains well why this should be so:

Christ's retirement to the wilderness is usually taken by the meditative handbooks as a symbol of the retirement of the soul to solitude for prayer and meditation: either actual solitude or 'spiritual retirement'. This seems to be the implication here: solitude, especially (for Vaughan) the solitude of nature, becomes a symbol for the spiritual retirement of the soul (the bride of Christ) in its devotions. Soon the one who so fervently seeks and asks will hear his answer. (p. 89)

And here Martz quotes most of the rest of the poem, from line 67 onward. We may perhaps supplement this account by suggesting that the placing of the reference to the wilderness at this transitional point of the poem enables the lyric with which the poem concludes to be more comprehensively suggestive than it would otherwise have been. The reader will notice that, whereas the greater part of the poem to this point embodies what we might call historical reference, the lyric suggests natural reference (*out of doors, the skin, and shell of things*); the reference to the wilderness enables these phrases to refer both to the 'externals' of biblical history which have provided the content of this poem so far, and also to the 'externals' of nature which provide the theme of other meditative poems of Vaughan. To a modern reader, it may seem like intellectual confusion for history and nature to be brought together in this way; it is perhaps worth recalling that in the orthodox Christian scheme to which Vaughan subscribed, history and nature were both conditioned by the Fall so that neither could yield anything but fragmentary truth to the senses of fallen man. Only by God's light shall we be able to see light. As Behmen says in his strange SIXTH EPISTLE which the reader of 'The Search' may well find suggestive for Behmen's concern about the 'externality' of most human knowing: *No knowledge is right or fundamental unless it comes from the divine science.*

Martz writes usefully of the lyric with which the poem ends:

The first stanza suggests that Christ is to be found within one's self; hence the phrase 'Search well another world' suggests the little world of man and the 'Manna', the eucharistic elements which when received, make Christ fully present within the little world (p. 90).

This interpretation would accord exactly with Vaughan's admonition, in his MOUNT OF OLIVES, to engage in careful self-examination as a preparation for reception of the Eucharist, for *such as our pre-disposition is, such also shall our proportion be of this spiritual* Manna (p. 90). The reference here to the reception of Christ in the sacrament offers a useful corrective to what I find is a fairly common way of reading the last three stanzas, which views them as, in effect, recommending a rather unfocused and subjective introspection. Nothing, I feel sure, could be further removed from Vaughan's intention in these three stanzas. For him, it was only insofar as God is present in the human mind (*a proportion of this spiritual* Manna) that man can be said to know anything at all, or as Behmen puts it in paragraph 61 of the SIXTH EPISTLE, *man is blind in all God's works, and hath no true knowledge, unless the Divine breathing . . . be revealed in his internal ground.*

A good way of ending one's reading of 'The Search', and one which Vaughan obviously intended, is to ponder the meaning and relevance of the quotation from Acts xvii 27—28 which Vaughan appends to it: *That they should seek the Lord, if happily they might feel after him, and find him, though he be not far off from every one of us, for in him we live, and move, and have our being.* Another is to return to the beginning of the poem and read it as if it were the end, a suggestion which the reader may find strange, but which is perhaps fair enough if we recall that the poem, so much of which refers to the historical past, begins in the present tense. On the one hand, as I have commented, Vaughan's writing gives to this meditation on the life of Christ a dramaticity and immediacy; on the other hand, the way in which the poem begins entitles us perhaps to think of it as *emotion recollected in tranquillity* or at all events as an account of a search of which the object has been attained. After a first reading too, we may find it relevant that the rose is, as Martz points out, the traditional symbol of the virgin, and we may well see a typical seventeenth-century pun in the reference to the Sun. At all events, the notion of pilgrimage in connection with Jesus can be found in Vaughan's prose:

Thy life here was nothing else but a pilgrimage and laborious search after sinners that thou mightst find them out and make them whole (M 161).

We might notice in these words an irony on which the poem may be said to be based, that it recalls a search for Him who has Himself sought out and found the searcher!

I have used Stanley Fish's phrase, and called the poem a self-consuming artifact. Does this mean that Vaughan simply repudiates the way of religious knowing on which most of the poem is based? I think not; more than one author has written to the effect that the attainment of knowledge is like climbing a ladder; one leaves the lower rungs behind, but this is not to deny their usefulness. The gradual attainment of knowledge of divine things might be said to be the theme of Dante's 'Paradiso'.

The reader wishing to think further about 'The Search' might consider two of its obvious contexts: George Herbert's poem of the same title is at least paradigmatically related to Vaughan's in its concern with the absence of God, which *doth excel / All distance known* and with His nearness which making two one *doth . . . bear the bell.* The biblical context suggested by the quotation appended to the poem is Acts xvii. In his sermon on Mars' hill, St. Paul argues against superstition; he tells his hearers that God dwells not in temples made with hands; and we are told, at the end of that chapter, that he converted Dionysius the Areopagite. This convert of St. Paul was the supposed author of several mystical treatises which Vaughan had almost certainly read (Thomas Vaughan quotes him in LUMEN DE LUMINE), and I suspect it would be worthwhile to examine the Dionysian writings with this particular poem in mind.

Patrick Grant, in THE TRANSFORMATION OF SIN, has written that 'Ascension Day' is not *much better than an adequate piece of versifying* and that it is not *particularly recognizable as being by Vaughan at all* (p. 145). I find this a quite extraordinary judgement, as it has always seemed to me quintessentially of Vaughan, and I cannot imagine it being ascribed by a sensitive reader to any other author. Look, for example, at the range of its biblical references. In the course of sixty-two lines there are allusions to all four gospels, to three epistles (James, Ephesians and II Corinthians), to Acts and to two Old Testament books, Genesis and Job. Then there is an obvious similarity in certain respects to 'The Search'; consider for example the way in which the first-person verbs (I saw, I greet and so on) animate and dramatize the meditation.

Above all, I think, the manner of the poem's natural references mark it as being by Vaughan:

Such was the bright world, on the first seventh day,
Before man brought forth sin, and sin decay;
When like a virgin clad in flowers *and* green
The pure earth sat, and the fair woods had seen
No frost, but flourished in that youthful vest,
With which their great Creator had them dressed.

This use of the word 'virgin' in reference to pre-lapsarian nature (here and in other poems such as 'The Night', and 'The Search', and 'Regeneration') is related to the language of Henry Vaughan's twin brother Thomas, as I have shown elsewhere ('Henry Vaughan and the Theme of Transfiguration': see the Bibliography). Vaughan's usage, which probably relates to Behmen as well as to Thomas Vaughan, focuses his sense that Nature as it was before the Fall, is still perceptible by regenerate man, and his related sense that the ordinary beauty of Nature, which even the unregenerate may enjoy, is the foretaste and as it were the guarantee of the final redemption of Nature. This matter, touched on in the fine eighth chapter of the Epistle to the Romans, though not taken up very much by western Christianity, was meaningful to the Orthodox Church of the East, and was important to Renaissance hermetists such as Paracelsus, Behmen, and the Vaughans. Of course, other Christian poets of the time referred to the innocence of Nature before the Fall, and Milton, in his 'Nativity Ode', writes of the order of the moment of creation being renewed at the time of Christ's birth. I cannot, however, think of any other seventeenth-century religious lyric poet whose preoccupation with a potentially transfigured nature equals that of Vaughan, so that, it seems to me, the references in this poem seem almost like a trade-mark.

Another element in the poem characteristic of Vaughan is the sense the reader has of the poet meditating out of doors, as in so many other poems of his, and seeing his own landscape as bathed in a biblical light; see for example lines 19–22:

> *I see that morning in thy Convert's tears,*
> *Fresh as the dew, which but this dawning wears!*
> *I smell her spices, and her ointment yields,*
> *As rich a scent as the now primrosed field.*

Again, one might refer to the eschatological ending of the poem, which can hardly be regarded as untypical of Vaughan!

Considering this poem as a meditation on the life of Christ, the reader will notice one significant difference from 'The Search': the importance of 'nature' in 'Ascension Day'. There is the long passage, already quoted in part, from line 30 to line 48; and there are other references which make us feel that this is very much a poem of Easter, which is not of course really incompatible with its title. We sense an atmosphere of personal regeneration, linked with the Resurrection, and with the spring which the poet is experiencing. Notice the sense of immediacy in phrases such as 'this dawning' (line 20), and 'the *now* primrosed fields'. When, in line 49, we read *With these fair thoughts I move in this fair place,* we are not sure whether the reference is to the biblical landscape in which Vaughan's imagination has been moving, or to the spring landscape which is presently before him. This sense of immediacy is further strengthened by the range of sensory references ('I see', line 19; 'I smell', line 21; 'I see them, hear them', line 30). The scholar may here fancy reminiscences of Behmen (*If God should account you worthy to have the light enkindled in your soul, you would see, taste, smell, feel and hear unspeakable words of God concerning this knowledge* [Epistle 32, paragraph 9]). But it is more important to sense that what Vaughan was experiencing in his here and now, in that particular spring, was enlivening his sense of the biblical passages on which he was meditating.

It is perhaps worth noticing the relaxed atmosphere of this poem, well suggested by the word 'mirth' at line 25. This fits the sense of assurance of his own salvation with which Vaughan opens the poem, which is not a record of searching, but rather a celebration of finding. Vaughan *greets* Christ's sepulchre, he does not seek for Christ there. In fact, the poem may be read as a joyful celebration of the meaning underlying the question *Why seek ye the living among the dead?* (Luke xxiv 15). The remarkable thing to me is that this is so literary and yet so intensely personal a poem.

In dealing with 'The Search', we noticed in Herbert's poem of the same title a reference to the sense of God's absence and to the sense of his presence. There are a number of indications in his poems that Vaughan experienced both extremes. This psychological experience is one he could have documented theologically from the hermetic books, where we find it stated that God is remote and unmanifest and at the same time *manifests himself ungrudgingly through the universe.* We often find in Vaughan the expression of the desire for the repetition of a spiritual experience, a contact with God which he feels he has experienced and lost again; we also find him repeatedly contemplating God in his works; if he could not reach to the Abyss of unmanifested deity in the prayer of union, he could come to a God *who art in all things, though invisibly* ('I walked the other day', line 54). More than any other aspect of hermetic theology it was the immanence of God in creation which most exercised Vaughan's imagination. That sense of God's immanence informs what is commonly thought of as being Vaughan's finest poem, 'The Night'. This poem has attracted much academic attention and scholars have discovered, or have thought that they have discovered, considerable complexities beneath its surface. It cannot be denied that there are genuine difficulties in detail which we become aware of as we attempt to read the poem with fuller understanding: what, for example, is the meaning of the phrase 'Virgin-shrine' in the poem's first line? What is the precise meaning of the simile of the glow-worms in the third line? And what is the simile in lines 50–52 telling us about the nature of the *deep but dazzling darkness* of God? While I would not belittle the work of scholars who have addressed themselves to these and other problems in the poem (I am among them), I think it would be a pity if its real or imagined complexities were to spoil our enjoyment of this beautiful lyric, which is surely the finest of Vaughan's meditations based upon the life of Christ.

Although 'The Night' is a meditation on the life of Christ, it takes the passage in the third chapter of St. John's gospel as starting point rather than as constant focus. If we compare it with 'The Search' or 'Ascension Day', it is clear that they have much more obvious biblical reference, or perhaps more accurately 'historical' reference to the material of the gospels. We might also conclude from the amount of scholarly writing on this particular poem, that as the historical reference has been pared to a minimum, there has been a corresponding increase in philosophical or theological reference, allusion, and implication. It is apparent from the title that Vaughan is taking as important for his own purposes the phrase 'by night' in the second verse of John iii; but he is not especially interested, at least not on the surface, in the 'historical' reason why Nicodemus came to Jesus by night: according to a contemporary commentator, John Diodati, *for fear of the* Jews' *persecution.* We feel, that is, that the poem is not merely a meditation on the life of Christ, but equally importantly a meditation on night, which may be read as a companion piece to 'The Morning-Watch'. As I want to consider 'The Night' in some detail, it will be necessary to quote:

Through that pure Virgin-shrine,
That sacred veil drawn o'er thy glorious noon

That men might look and live as glow-worms shine,
And face the moon:
Wise Nicodemus *saw such light*
As made him know his God by night.

I have argued elsewhere that the phrase 'Virgin-shrine' refers both to the night sky and to the earthly body of Christ. I remarked in my edition that the night sky contains the moon, Diana, *Queen and Huntress, chaste and fair,* but failed to notice a possibly relevant iconographical connection, between the moon and the Virgin Mary, who is referred to in the first line of Vaughan's poem 'The Knot' as *bright Queen of Heaven.* One iconographical representation of Mary in renaissance art portrays her as Queen of Heaven; she is pictured standing on the crescent moon crowned as Queen. Frequently the crown bears the twelve stars of the apocalyptic vision: see Revelation xii 1.

The application of the phrase 'Virgin-shrine' to Christ in his human existence is complex and the interested reader should refer to my article in the MODERN LANGUAGE REVIEW. The fact that the phrase does refer to the body of Christ is indicated by its being in apposition to 'That sacred veil' in the second line which presumably refers to *the veil, that is to say, his flesh* in Hebrews x 20. As the night itself may be thought of as veiling the Sun from men's eyes, so the body of Christ may be thought of as paradoxically both revealing and concealing God in him. The phrase 'thy glorious noon' implies the traditional image of Christ as the Son of Righteousness. We must remember that as man cannot look with naked eye upon the sun, so *no man hath seen God at any time* (John i 18) and *who sees God's face, that is self life, must die* (Donne, 'Goodfriday 1613. Riding Westward'). Commentators have found considerable difficulty with the simile of the glow-worms in lines 3 and 4. I think it might help to remember the purpose of the simile, that is to indicate why a veil has to be drawn over the noon of Christ. It is for the reasons indicated by the quotations from the Bible and from Donne that I have just given: man cannot directly look at God; but Christ was *the image of the invisible God* (Colossians i 15). The earthly body of Christ therefore might be taken as analogous to the night sky which veils the sun but reveals the moon, which as Genesis i 16 reminds us is the *lesser light to rule the night.* As glow-worms cannot shine in the presence of sunlight so man could not live in the direct presence of God. I think it is worthwhile drawing attention to a fruitful ambiguity in the third line: on the one hand the words 'look' and 'live' have as it were their merely biological meanings; on the other they may be read on a more spiritual level, in which case 'look' refers to the spiritual perception with which man recognizes the Godhead in Christ and 'live' refers not just to biological existence but to the kind of life which Vaughan characterizes in another poem as *a quickness, which my God hath kissed* and which refers back to Christ's own saying *I am come that they might have life, and that they might have it more abundantly* (John x 10).

2

Most blest believer he!
Who in that land of darkness and blind eyes

Thy long expected healing wings could see,
When thou didst rise,
And what can never more be done,
Did at mid-night speak with the Sun!

3
O who will tell me, where
He found thee at that dead and silent hour!
What hallowed solitary ground did bear
So rare a flower,
Within whose sacred leaves did lie
The fullness of the Deity.

We may compare with the second stanza a passage from Behmen: *there is a wonderful time coming, but because it beginneth in the night, there are many that shall not see it, by reason of their sleep and drunkenness; yet the Sun will shine on the Children at Midnight* (Preface to the Reader, THE THREE PRINCIPLES OF THE DIVINE ESSENCE, English translation, 1648). I offer this quotation, not necessarily as a source, but as a striking analogue. It seems likely, given what we know from other contexts of Vaughan's view of the spiritual state of England in his time, that he had his own country, as well as that of Jesus, in mind when he wrote the second line of stanza two; and that consideration helps to lend poignancy to the question which begins stanza three. In annotating this poem I commented that its imagery does not evoke Christ as an historical personage, but the notion of the cosmic Christ, in which the stress is upon Christ's immanence in natural phenomena, rather than upon a particular historical and personal manifestation. I am grateful to a correspondent who pointed out to me the relevance of Isaiah liii 2 *for he shall grow up before him as a tender plant, and as a root out of dry ground.* The context in Isaiah makes it clear that this passage is one of those taken as prophetically referring to Christ. Also relevant is the Christian myth of the Tree of Life, referred to obliquely in Vaughan's poem 'St. Mary Magdalen' in the beautiful lines *That at the root of this green tree/Thy great decays restored might be.* As so often in Vaughan, the image (of Christ as a flower) has its primary source in the Bible, but here its potency for Vaughan seems to have been enhanced by post-biblical speculations.

The question which begins stanza three relates directly to the subject of 'The Search', which as I have suggested is central to post-Reformation thinking on the nature of Christ. Vaughan's answer then should be taken with some seriousness:

4

No mercy-seat of gold,
No dead and dusty Cherub, *nor carved stone,*
But his own living works did my Lord hold
And lodge alone;
Where trees *and* herbs *did watch and peep*
And wonder, while the Jews *did sleep.*

Behind this stanza is the story of Solomon's building and consecrating the Temple (I Kings) and that of the supersession of the Temple by Christ (Epistle to the Hebrews, especially chapter 9). In the phrase *his own living works* there seems to be a glancing reference to Hebrews ix 14, where we are told how the blood of Christ purges the conscience from dead works to serve the living God. But the 'works' of stanza four are not deeds of men, but the works of God in the creation. On the literal level the stanza might be taken as saying simply that Jesus was to be found in the open air, but I think most readers would agree that the expression suggests more than this, that the spirit of Christ informed the natural scene, was immanent within it, making it seem natural that spiritual awareness should be seen in the *trees* and *herbs* while the Jews remained asleep. In this respect the stanza goes beyond its 'source' in Hebrews and answers in a radical way Solomon's question at the consecration of the Temple: *But will God indeed dwell on the earth? Behold, the Heaven and Heaven of Heavens cannot contain thee; how much less this house that I have builded?* (I Kings viii 27). It is in this context of Christ's indwelling in His creation that we should understand the rhapsodic apostrophe 'Dear night!' which introduces stanzas five and six, which may be read as a series of descriptions leading up to the statement of the seventh stanza. The *dyfalu* of stanza five has been judged *out of keeping* (Pettet); to me it seems to prepare for the great sixth stanza in which we again apprehend night as place rather than as time:

6

God's silent, searching flight:
When my Lord's head is filled with dew, and all
His locks are wet with the clear drops of night;
His still, soft call;
His knocking time; the soul's dumb watch,
When Spirits their fair kindred catch.

In commenting on 'The Search' I wrote that it recalls a search for Him who has himself sought out and found the searcher. We might notice here the quietly unobtrusive answer to the emphatic question of stanza three; God's is a *searching* flight.

It is typical of Vaughan that this poem, in the very ecstasy of its expression, should assure us that its author attained a sense of close communion with God; typical too that he should explicitly disclaim any ability to remain more than momentarily upon the mystical heights. That disclaimer is here the subject of stanzas seven and eight; but *aesthetically* we may see the slackening of those stanzas as skilful preparation for the splendid prayer with which the poem closes:

9

There is in God (some say)
A deep, but dazzling darkness; as men here
Say it is late and dusky, because they
See not all clear;
O for that night! Where I in him
Might live invisible and dim.

In this final stanza Vaughan returns to the play on light and darkness which animates the beginning of the poem. The *deep but dazzling darkness* of God is based upon a passage in Dionysius the Areopagite, which Thomas Vaughan refers to in LUMEN DE LUMINE: *The divine darkness is unapproachable light, in which God is said to dwell.* The simile beginning at line fifty is not easy. A recent suggestion is that the lateness referred to is the lateness of time itself, that is, the nearness of the Day of Judgement. Unfortunately this view fails to explain how the lines function as simile, how they illustrate the statement about the darkness of God. It seems to me that we should rather think of the fact that men here, with their limited vision, which is akin to the limited vision of those who ascribe *deep but dazzling darkness* to God, say it is dusky because their vision is obscured by the earth, as it turns on its axis and obscures the sun. If we were not earth-bound, we would experience a light so dazzling that it would perhaps seem to us like a darkness. This explanation has the merit of exact congruence with the Dionysian paradoxes which occur through the poem, re-surfacing at the beginning of the final stanza, since Dionysius insists that men must transcend all phenomena, into *the beam of the godly darkness.*

Death, Judgement, Heaven and Hell in Vaughan's Poems

Meditation on death has long been recognized as important to the religious sensibility of the early seventeenth century. One way to analyze how poets of the period differ from one another might be to compare their treatments of death, and of the other subjects of Christian eschatology: judgement, heaven and hell. Donne's addresses to God the Father in his HOLY SONNETS, for example, differ considerably from anything we find in Vaughan.

Vaughan's treatment of eschatological themes is at times remarkably idiosyncratic; indeed, some of the beliefs he expresses had been proclaimed false, for example by Aquinas, in the Middle Ages; and they were again proclaimed false, in the very different circumstances of Vaughan's own time, for example by Thomas Edwards in his GANGRAENA, a catalogue of sectarian heresies in England during the period of the Civil War, published in 1646. I am referring to his theme of *apokatastasis,* or the restoration of all things, a theme merely hinted at in the New Testament and made more of by Vaughan than by any other religious poet of the time. Idiosyncratic too is the way in which Vaughan's emotional drive towards unity expresses itself in his treatment of eschatological themes. In his *motifs* of potentiality and of transfiguration (alchemical and otherwise) we may descry an original extension of the New Testament concepts of the Kingdom of God as hidden, as present and as to come; and we may see Vaughan working out these themes in terms of epistemology (his implied theory of knowledge) and of eschatology (his view of the final state of things). I have shown elsewhere how Vaughan's treatment of these themes relates to his reading: of hermetic authors such as Behmen, Paracelsus, Agrippa; and of the hermetic *libelli.* While it may be necessary to touch upon hermeticism again, it is important that we should think of Vaughan's characteristic treatment of these themes, not simply in terms of literary influences, but rather with a view to the way in which they point us to the leading tendencies of his mind: his mind, that is, considered not merely as a repository of literature, but as a system of energies seeking to stabilize itself. It is in this light that we shall examine the desire for unity and the theme of restoration as they appear in his eschatological verse.

That eschatological themes should be prominent in Vaughan's verse is not in itself surprising; from the times of the very earliest Christians, who had expected the imminent Parousia, or return of Christ in glory, through the Middle Ages, when many had looked forward to the thousand years reign of Christ, down to the Reformation, men had looked forward in various ways to the end of history as we know it, when God would vindicate himself against his enemies and justify the elect. In Vaughan's own time, the emotional impact of the Civil War was such as to make it likely that the eschatological element in Christianity would once again become prominent. As the Israelites of the Babylonian captivity had yearned for their return to Jerusalem and the rebuilding of the Temple, so sensitive Anglicans, living through the spiritual captivity of the Cromwellian regime, must have comforted themselves with the thought that their enemies were also God's enemies, and that eventually God must vindicate Himself and restore the faithful. We tend to forget that for almost the whole of the period between 1649 and 1660 it must have seemed unlikely that the Monarchy and the Church of England would be restored during the lifetime of men then living. The very harshness of the times, for Royalists and Anglicans, would have led the more religiously inclined of them to expect the end of all things, for it was part of Old

Testament prophetic teaching that the Day of Judgement would be heralded by various woes, after which would come the Day of the Lord when God would vindicate Himself against the sinful nation.

I want for a moment to think of these matters psychologically rather than theologically or in terms of conventional literary or historical criticism. Considered in these terms it seems likely that intensely painful experiences occurring in the public realm (for example, the Civil War, the judicial murder of Charles I, the dismantling of the Established Church) might exacerbate individual conflicts within the personality and call forth a correspondingly intense reaction, given a sufficient symbolic correspondence between these public events and painful early experiences; and it seems likely that Vaughan's documentably intense reaction to the Civil War fits such a pattern. We don't have enough biographical information to document Vaughan's early experiences. One might suspect, though, that the intensity of his grief at William's death points to a significant component of guilt arising from Henry's early relationship with his younger brother; it may be that his removal from home to reside with Matthew Herbert at the age of eleven or so was important. What seems fairly clear from the intensity of his response to the public events of his early manhood is that those events touched upon something very painful in his personality.

Psychologists tell us that when adults idealize the state of childhood (as Vaughan may be said to do in 'Child-hood' and 'The Retreat') the likelihood is that their actual childhoods were filled with pain and loss, the memory of which has been suppressed. Experiences of early loss cause emotional damage which the mind, a self-righting mechanism, then seeks to repair. Adult experiences which are intensely painful are so, according to psychologists, because they symbolically reproduce the most intensely painful experiences of childhood. Early losses might be symbolically repaired by attachment to figures and institutions, symbolizing loving authority, in Vaughan's case, the King and the Church. The forceful apparent destruction of these institutions, to which he clung so intensely, would lead to a renewal of the anguish which had accompanied the original loss. When the *institutional* attachments by which repair has been effected are broken, then this second loss can only be repaired symbolically in the private realm. For a writer, this will mean that the personality's drive to re-integration will be expressed in the patterns and structures he can conjure up with words: we might look for a strong rejection of painful elements, and a drive to make pattern and unity out of phenomena, the apparent diversity of which will tend to mirror painfully the fragmentation within the psyche attendant upon traumatic loss. The Civil War and the execution of Charles I would thus be quite sufficient to explain the 'conversion' which turned the author of POEMS 1646 and OLOR ISCANUS into the poet of SILEX SCINTILLANS; and in Vaughan's case we might see the negative aspect of this psychic programme in the implicit rejection of the social from his poetic vision. There are a few poems addressed to close friends, and there are a number of fine elegies, but people who have *gone into the world of light* are not inhabitants of a society of this world! Otherwise, where the world is noticed in Vaughan's poetry at all, it is with scorn and dislike as in 'The World' and 'The Proffer'. As his imagination, working within the general outline of Christian eschatology, remade the world to his own liking, the punishment of God's (and his) enemies occurs, it is true, but more pervasive, significant and characteristic are the positive elements in his vision. This is in keeping with New Testament eschatology, which lays stress on the hope of the righteous rather than on the doom of the wicked.

The foregoing generalizations must be tested by looking at what actually happens in the poems. The four last things are Death, Judgement, Heaven and Hell. Imilda Tuttle's CONCORDANCE enables us fairly rapidly to examine all the occurrences of the word 'death' in SILEX SCINTILLANS. To do this is to be re-assured that the negative connotations of 'death' are almost always cancelled out contextually. The quotation that comes first to my mind when thinking about Vaughan on death is that from 'Resurrection and Immortality':

And how of death we make
A mere mistake,
For no thing can to Nothing *fall.*

This is a denial of death's reality, admittedly from an immediate context which owes more to hermetic theorising on the function of the World-Soul than it does to Christian teaching on the efficacy of Christ's sacrifice and Resurrection (the language of the poem's ending is Christian enough). Of course one instance does not establish a tendency. The third stanza of 'The Check' is another good example; we are told (in a verbal progression that is itself characteristic and interesting and will be examined later) that *birds, beasts, each tree/All that have growth, or breath/Have one large language,* Death. Death is universal and there is a lesson to be learned from that fact. The lesson is that we must 'strive to' God:

Whose power doth so excel
As to make clay
A spirit, and true glory dwell
In dust, and stones.

The end of this stanza, in which God is said to make *true glory dwell/In dust, and stones* suggests that Vaughan is not merely advising his fellow-men to take warning from the death of *birds, beasts, each tree* and so ensure their personal immortality: the entire physical creation is open to God's transfiguring and eternizing power, as St. Paul argues in Romans viii 21: *the creature itself also shall be delivered from the bondage of corruption into the glorious liberty of the children of God.*

Vaughan's reactions to the events of his own life (grief at the death of his brother and some of his friends, illness, destruction of monarchy and Church) suggests that he was severely threatened by depression at one stage. Depression classically entails an immobility, an inability to act constructively or creatively, for which death might be an appropriate metaphor. The poems of SILEX SCINTILLANS are the result of the energies he summoned and deployed to propel himself away from that immobility: it is not through a merely conventional use of religious language I think that the adjective 'dead' is applied to his own heart, or that he sees God and Christ as exercising a miracle upon his heart parallel to the Resurrection of Christ. God's vivifying powers are celebrated in a number of places: in 'The Jews' the Holy Spirit (*the bright* Dove) is seen as able to make *living waters flow/To make dry dust, and dead trees grow.* In his paraphrase of Psalms 104, he says, addressing God, *The frozen earth's dead face thou dost renew.* In 'Jesus Weeping' (I) he asks Christ to *pour this latter/Soul-quickening rain, this living water/On their dead hearts.* In 'Jesus Weeping' (II) the breath of Christ *can make man's dead and scattered bones/Unite, and raise up all that died, at once.* (Note the theme of multiplicity tending towards unity.) We find that when the adjective 'dead' or the noun 'death' occur in Vaughan's poems it is almost invariably in a context which recalls the life-giving power of God or the life-giving sacrifice of Christ. Moreover, death does not have that positive reality for Vaughan that led Donne, for example, to personify it in the sonnet beginning *Death be not proud, though some have called thee/Mighty and dreadful;* he does not, even for dramatic emphasis, need to aggrandize death in order to make a point about the efficacy of Christ's conquest of death. Whatever fears one might descry in Vaughan's work, the fear of death is not among them. In 'They are all gone into the world of light!' he exclaims *Dear, beauteous death! the jewel of the just* and says of those he is remembering *They are all gone into the world of light!* We might contrast this with Wordsworth's use of this image in reverse in his 'Extempore Effusion upon the death of James Hogg': *How fast has brother followed brother,/From sunshine to the sunless land!* or with the muted and qualified optimism of the ending of his 'Elegaic Stanzas, suggested by a picture of Peele Castle': *Not without hope we suffer and we mourn.* Vaughan's attitude to death indeed at times becomes an absolute yearning: in 'Cock-Crowing', referring to the veil of the flesh, he prays *O take it off,* while 'They are all gone into the world of light!' ends:

Either disperse these mists, which blot and fill
My perspective (still) as they pass,
Or else remove me hence unto that hill,
Where I shall need no glass.

As we have seen, then, the words 'death' and 'dead' in Vaughan's verse almost invariably occur in a context which emphasizes the vivifying power of God and the redemptive power of Christ. If we consider the second term in the eschatological series, Judgement, we find that it is not listed in Imilda Tuttle's CONCORDANCE as occurring in SILEX; 'judge' and 'judging' do occur but far less frequently than 'death' and 'dead'. This, taken together with what we have perceived of the contextualized meaning of 'death' and 'dead', seems to support what has already been suggested, that the negative aspect of the eschatological theme (God's judgement upon the wicked) looms less large for Vaughan than does the positive, as is the case in the New Testament. This is true, I think, though the negative aspect has its importance and should not be played down.

Vaughan has two poems obviously and explicitly on this theme. 'Day of Judgement' occurs near the beginning of SILEX I, 'The Day of Judgement' near the end of SILEX II. The first, using the traditional biblical imagery (mainly from Revelation) deals with the destruction of the world and the summoning of the souls of the dead:

When thou shalt make the clouds thy seat,
And in the open air
The quick, and dead, both small and great
Must to thy bar repair;

O then it will be all too late
To say, What shall I do?
Repentance *there is out of date*
And so is mercy *too.*

It is tempting to read this as one of the saved admonishing sinners, or perhaps as the Royalist Anglican threatening the regicide persecutors of his Church; but in fact Vaughan is looking closer to home. This stanza is closely related to the ending of Donne's 'Holy Sonnet' *(At the round earth's imagined corners),* where, having looked forward with relish to the Day of Judgement, the poet continues on a more sombre note in the sestet:

For, if above all these, my sins abound,
'Tis late to ask abundance of thy grace,

When we are there; here on this lowly ground,
Teach me how to repent.

In Vaughan's poem as in Donne's, the need for repentance is felt personally, as the following stanzas make clear:

Prepare, prepare me then, O God!
And let me now begin
To feel my loving Father's rod
Killing the man of sin!

Give me, O give me crosses here,
Still more afflictions lend,
That pill, though bitter, is most dear
That brings health in the end.

Here the poet realizes that he is himself a sinner; and the 'afflictions' of his own present are seen within the framework of God's mercies. The Old Testament notion that the responsible parent will chastise his children *(Spare the rod and spoil the child)* is here taken from its merely human context and referred to the relationship between God and man. Affliction, whatever its immediate source (sickness or the hostile acts of an enemy) is seen as God's chastisement: the feelings of helplessness and depression attendant upon such afflictions are transmuted to Christian humility and the affliction, seen as deserved chastisement, is accepted and indeed embraced; and in the final stanza of the poem the enmity of the world is seen as keeping 'fresh' a living Faith, a heart of flesh. The 'crosses' of the present are chastisements that God intends to ensure that the final irrevocable doom will not be visited upon the child he loves.

The corresponding poem in SILEX II is very different, and perhaps rather less successful in that its ideas are strung together rather than achieving organic coherence. At first it stresses the joyful aspect of the day of judgement:

O day of life, of light, of love!
The only day dealt from above!
A day so fresh, so bright, so brave
'Twill show us each forgotten grave,
And make the dead, like flowers, arise
Youthful and fair to see new skies.

The vocabulary of this is typical of Vaughan and so perhaps are the exclamatory mode of the opening (which is an ironic echo of the 'Dies Irae') and the sense of longing for the end of things. Typical too is the sense that God's mercies extend to the non-human creation, expressed in lines 15–16; *My fellow-creatures too say,* Come!/ *And stones, though speechless, are not dumb;* so also is the effective collocation of the concrete word and the abstraction in the lines *Shall bring true day, and make dust see,/The way to immortality.* From line 27 however, the writing seems to grow somewhat slack, as Vaughan turns away from the bright vision of the end to the darker view of the present. It is not that the sins of the present time are irrelevant, but rather that Vaughan's specificity in the references to:

The vile despite done to thy name;
The forgeries, which impious wit
And power force on Holy Writ,

suggest ecclesiastical wrangling rather than the grandeur of a larger vision. Except for the final line the prayer which ends the poem (from line 39 on) may be read as a request to God to act against Vaughan's enemies.

These two poems represent what one might call a centrally orthodox treatment of eschatology, different as each is from the other. Beyond them, it should be stressed that reference to the Day of Judgement is pervasive in both parts of SILEX SCINTILLANS; a great many of Vaughan's poems end with prayer, and of these many pray for the Day of Judgement to be accomplished. 'Burial' ends: *Lord haste, Lord come,/O come Lord* Jesus *quickly!* echoing Revelation. 'Rules and Lessons' ends with a summary of its teaching *(Do as thou wouldst be done unto,/Love God, and love thy neighbour; watch, and pray)* and a warning to those who do not follow it *(who doth not thus, hath lost Heaven's way)* reinforced by the grim question, *wilt change those* lights/*For* chains *of* darkness, *and* eternal nights? Given that Vaughan's contemporary readers would have caught biblical allusions more readily than most twentieth-century readers, it is worth recalling the source of this: *God spared not the angels that sinned, but cast them down to hell, and delivered them unto chains of darkness, to be reserved unto judgement* (2 Peter ii 4). The finality of God's doom upon unrepentant sinners could hardly be made clearer: they will be damned as utterly and as surely as the rebellious angels.

The ending of 'Corruption' helps to illustrate the way in which Christians living in bad times could comfort themselves with the thought of the Day of Judgement. The prophets had taught that *the Day of the Lord* would be preluded by various woes, and this teaching was taken up into Christian eschatology; see for example the so-called 'Little Apocalypse' of Mark, where the point is made that the discerning will be able to recognize the imminence of judgement by the woes: *So ye . . . when ye shall see these things come to pass, know that it is night,* even *at the doors* (Mark xiii 29). Some of the woes forecast in this chapter must have seemed to many in the seventeenth century prophetic of their own time. The Civil War must have caused them to ponder verse 12: *Now the brother shall betray the brother to death, and the father the son; and children shall rise up against their parents;* and the religious ferment of the 1640s would have recalled verse 22: *For false Christs and false prophets shall arise.* My first point is that, whereas today belief in the imminence of the Day of Judgement is confined to comparatively small sects, which are regarded as heretical by Christians of the major denominations, in those days such beliefs existed across the spectrum of Christian believers. The second point is that, by a comforting paradox, the worse the times, the more apparently hopeless the age, the nearer the Day of Judgement *must* be, so that an external situation apparently conducive to despair is transformed, when viewed eschatologically, into a time of hope. Perhaps such periods, by their very intensity, tend to be brief; but one may imagine that pondering upon the Day of Judgement helped Vaughan through the worst days of the interregnum, or so the ending of 'Corruption', with its reference to Revelation xiv 18, would suggest:

Sin triumphs still, and man is sunk below
The centre, and his shroud;

All's in deep sleep, and night; thick darkness lies
And hatcheth o'er thy people;
But hark! what trumpet's that? what Angel cries
Arise! Thrust in thy sickle.

The possible *imminence* of the Day of Judgement is again touched upon at the end of 'The Check':

Redeem the day,
The day that gives no observation,
Perhaps tomorrow.

The preceding three or four examples are from SILEX I; there are many more in the second part of SILEX, so that we can say that Vaughan's habit of thinking eschatologically did not weaken between 1650 and 1655. We should expect the references to the Day of Judgement that occur in 'Ascension-Day' and 'Ascension-Hymn', because Christ's Second Coming is foretold in the account of His ascension (Acts i 9–11); but in 'The Rain-bow' too Vaughan meditates on this sign *that seed-time and harvest shall not fail* (see Genesis viii 22 and ix 8–17) and sees it as presaging judgement: *I know well, and so our sins require,/Thou dost but court cold rain, till* rain *turns* fire.

In 'The Seed Growing Secretly', as elsewhere (for example, in 'The Book'), Vaughan links the themes of hiddenness, of potentiality, and of judgement:

Then bless thy secret growth, nor catch
At noise, but thrive unseen and dumb;
Keep clean, bear fruit, earn life and watch
Till the white winged Reapers come!

Before I go on to consider Vaughan's more idiosyncratic references to eschatological themes, it is perhaps worth saying that here as elsewhere a reader's biblical awareness can avoid misreadings. In line 13 of 'The British Church', for example, 'the day' refers to the Day of Judgement and 'Discipline' has been misread by scholars partly because they failed to realize the significance of its background in 2 Peter, so that they read the phrase 'thy day' naturalistically rather than as reference to the Day of the Lord.

This chapter has already dealt with Death and Judgement; the other two of the four last things are Heaven and Hell. Vaughan's treatment of judgement is comparatively conventional: his ideas would be readily understood and accepted by almost all instructed Christians of his time. His view of death, as we have seen, is far more individual; and closely linked with this are his views of Hell and Heaven, or rather his view of the ultimate fate of the human soul; for Vaughan is not much concerned with the traditional notions of Heaven and Hell, as describable in terms of place. His view of the ultimate destiny of the soul is closely connected with several of his most characteristic themes.

The themes or *motifs* that converge in Vaughan's eschatological poems are highly characteristic and personal; to consider them together is to arrive at a sense of what it is that gives Vaughan such distinctiveness as a poet (one recognizes of course that his distinctiveness inheres not merely in themes but also in tone, rhythm and so on). To consider these themes together is also to see how they are related one to the other, to have a sense of the way in which they cohered within Vaughan's mind, the way in which for him they constituted what might be called a cosmos of meaning won by meditation from the random multiplicity of experience.

I have noticed elsewhere the theme or motif of potentiality in Vaughan's work, and connected this with the theme of hiddenness. Vaughan is concerned, not with mere external phenomena, not with mere appearance, but with the possibility of growth, regeneration, transfiguration in that which is scarcely visible and scarcely seen to be alive. This theme of Vaughan's may be connected with his eschatological thought if we consider the hermetic extension of the Aristotelian concept of entelechy, the view that each thing contains within itself the seed of its own proper perfection. So, the entelechy of the acorn is the full-grown oak tree. However, a Christian hermetist like Vaughan would take the concept of entelechy beyond a purely naturalistic setting. For him, the ultimate entelechy of the acorn would not be the oak tree available to man's ordinary perception, but rather the oak tree as it flourishes in a world from which death and decay have been purged. As Paracelsus remarks, each individual flower has its place in eternity. It was in this belief that the Renaissance hermetist differed from a traditionally orthodox theologian such as Aquinas. There is, of course, a biblical source both for Vaughan's philosophy of potentiality and for its connection with his thinking on the last things; I mean the parables of sowing that we find in the gospels, especially perhaps such a parable as that of the seed growing secretly (Mark iv 26), for in these parables the seed (potentiality) is connected with harvest (realization) and of course the harvest is in the gospel the metaphor for the Day of Judgement. It refers to the day when God will gather His crop and will destroy the weeds that have grown up alongside it. As I have shown, this theme of potentiality can be seen in such poems as 'Rules and Lessons' and 'I walked the other day'.

Closely related to the theme or philosophy of potentiality is Vaughan's theme of transfiguration, which I have discussed elsewhere in connection with the poem 'Regeneration'; in fact it might be asked whether the theme of transfiguration is not merely the theme of potentiality under a different name. The object transfigured is perhaps identical to the object with its potentiality fully realized. Certainly I think that both themes (if they may be distinguished) are connected with a Jungian sense of the regenerative possibilities inherent in the subconscious mind. As worked out explicitly in Vaughan's poetry and in the writings of some Renaissance hermetic philosophers, the theme of transfiguration may be connected with an interest in alchemy, and with a philosophy of perception, as well as with the theme of eschatology. Perhaps one way of indicating a useful distinction between the two themes is to suggest that the theme of potentiality as it occurs within Vaughan's poetry has a mainly human bearing, even though the images by which it is expressed may be images drawn from the non-human world, as in the 'poor root' of 'I walked the other day'. The theme of transfiguration may be seen as related or parallel, but as applying to the natural world as well as to the world of the human. I have suggested a connection between the themes of potentiality and hiddenness and New Testament notions of the Kingdom of God such as are conveyed in the parables of seeds and sowing. Vaughan extends this idea into the natural world: the cleansing, healing, and fructifying work of the Kingdom is enlarged from the merely human to the entire natural universe, so that, running parallel with the regeneration of man is, so to say, a preparation for *the new heaven and the new earth,* of which the Bible speaks, but which had not been taken very seriously in orthodox Western theology. That is, Vaughan appears to have taken seriously the possibility of a transfigured natural world such as is hinted at by St. Paul: *the creature itself also shall be delivered from the bondage of corruption into the glorious liberty of the children of God* (Romans viii 21).

In Vaughan, as in such hermetic philosophers as Paracelsus and Agrippa, the theme of transfiguration is frequently conveyed through alchemical imagery, as in 'The Sap' and 'St. Mary Magdalen', for of course, transformation or transfiguration was precisely the object of the alchemist's search. Behind alchemical practice was the theory that everything in the universe is slowly moving towards a perfection proper to itself. Man's striving for spiritual perfection and the metals' slow ripening into gold were felt as analogies because they were conceived of as being manifestations of the same cosmic process taking place on different levels of existence. The action of the 'tincture' on impure metals and that of Christ in the human personality were, again, felt to be one and the same action operating on two different levels. Man was thought of by the alchemists as being nature's high priest; his task was to help effect the *transfiguration of the cosmos.* In a sense the idea of the transfiguration of the cosmos enters into hermetic epistemology as a theory of perception (the pre-lapsarian world is available here and now to the senses of the regenerate man); but we would not know from that how literally the hermetists believed in the possibility of transfiguration. It enters too into the hermetic eschatology; the whole universe, cleansed and transformed, is to be drawn into the presence of God: we shall see such ideas at work in a later discussion of 'The Book'. Vaughan's brother Thomas was a practising alchemist and Vaughan says in a letter *my profession is also in physic;* his interest in the alchemical ideas of Renaissance hermetists is documentable from his prose works. Carl Jung's PSYCHOLOGY AND ALCHEMY shows how, psychologically, the search for gold objectifies man's desire for perfection, with the philosopher's stone often representing Christ, the tincture which works the miracle of the transmutation of base lives. We might say then that Vaughan's working out of the theme of transfiguration in various contexts in his poetry represents psychologically a drive towards harmony, beauty, cleanness, that is, towards a mental state and a physical universe from which all that is merely random and all that is distressing or painful has been purged away. There is a connection too between the theme of transfiguration in Vaughan's work and that of the innocence of childhood expressed in for instance 'The Retreat' and 'Child-hood'; that is, a connection between Vaughan's nostalgia on the one hand and his aspirations on the other, a connection between the ideas of original innocence and final innocence. Philosophically the two themes may be connected by the consideration that in Vaughan's philosophy of pre-existence, the soul, like everything else in the universe, came from God and is destined to return to God. Psychologically at all events there is a clear connection at the simplest level in that, whether he is looking back toward childhood or looking forward to his perfected state in the eternal world, Vaughan is concerned with integrity, with a state from which all that is evil and all that is painful has been purged.

In a notable SCRUTINY essay on the metaphysical poets, James Smith remarked that these poets are metaphysical in the true sense, because they are concerned with the relationship between the One and the Many. Smith takes Donne as his principal example but as I have suggested elsewhere the remark applies equally well to Vaughan. The language of his poems, and perhaps especially notably the language in eschatological contexts, clearly demonstrates what one might term a drive towards unity. This is so marked that it may be taken as a distinctive characteristic of Vaughan's mental dynamic; and like the theme of transfiguration this theme of unity too can be connected with the activities of the alchemists. As well as searching for gold, alchemists searched for the *prima materia,* that is, the hidden matter which is as it were the unperceived base of all phenomena, and this search for the *prima materia* represents man's efforts to pierce through the multiplicity of sense-objects to the underlying reality. Philosophically, it may be described as the application of a metaphysical idealism to a philosophy of nature; psychologically, it seems to be bound up with a condition known as 'cosmic consciousness', a condition resulting from an *upheaval of the subconscious mind . . . uncovering . . . those layers of memory which record the experiences of pre-natal life. Such a glimpse would seem to . . . reveal the unity underlying all the life of nature* (Elizabeth Holmes, HENRY VAUGHAN AND THE HERMETIC PHILOSOPHY, p. 19).

Whereas many seventeenth-century thinkers seem to have considered the world to be in a state of decay, the hermetic philosophers, and to judge by his poems Vaughan among them, thought of the universe as being in a state of creative evolution with God working intimately in all things and man assisting (by priestly scientific activity for the alchemists and by a life of virtue for the religious poet) in the divine purpose. The contrary idea of nature as being depraved since the Fall is of course Pauline and Augustinian (though Paul, as in the passage from Romans viii 21 already quoted, does hold out hope for the transfiguration of nature through the mediation of regenerate mankind). Hermeticism then, especially perhaps on its scientific side, was an optimistic philosophy compared with the view generally current in the early seventeenth century. A melancholy man such as Henry Vaughan seems to have been, might well be attracted, in a period of personal and political depression, to a world view expressive of a cosmic optimism.

Alexander Grosart, one of Vaughan's nineteenth-century editors, said of Vaughan that *He makes us feel that Nature is not a mere collection of phenomena, but infuses into her least approach some sense of her mysterious whole.* (Incidentally, A. N. Whitehead made a similar statement about Wordsworth in SCIENCE AND THE MODERN WORLD: *He always grasps the whole of nature as involved in the tonality of the particular instance.*) As was suggested earlier, Vaughan is concerned about the relationship between the One and the Many; I want now to look at this theme of multiplicity and unity, which is closely related to the themes of potentiality and transfiguration.

There is an interesting and characteristic verbal progression in the third stanza of 'The Check': *birds, beasts, each tree/All that have growth, or breath/Have one large language,* Death. We see that this passage begins with plurals ('birds, beasts') and ends with a singular ('Death') which is emphasized as such by the word 'one'. The phrase 'each tree' is more than merely a different kind of plural thrown in to fill out the metre of the line.

OED defines 'each' as *every (individual of a number) reported or treated separately.* It is related to the word 'every' which was in Old English 'ever each' (âefre âelc) and which is *used to express distributively the sense that is expressed collectively by* all. The point here is that the word 'each' includes in its meaning both the idea of *individuality* and that of participation in a family or group. We might say that its meaning points to the tension between the one and the many; that if used with the stress on *individuality* it points towards *multiplicity* (because there are many individuals in a family or group); whereas if the stress is upon participation in the family then we are pointed towards unity (because the individuals are sustained within one family). In this particular progression of words the differences between birds, beasts, and trees are subsumed within the initial word of the line *All that have growth, or breath:* as if there is one family of living things, a unity which is emphasized in the following line *Have one large language,* Death. On one level what this means is that all mortal creatures have one overwhelming lesson to teach man, that *all that lives must die*. But on another we might see Death as a metaphor for the unity to which all multiplicity leads. (*The one remains, the many change and pass* was Shelley's formulation of this piece of Platonism). The kind of verbal progression we have here may also be found in St. Paul's thinking about the relationship between Christians, Christ and God, as in I Corinthians 21–23: *For all things are yours . . . And ye are Christ's; and Christ is God's.* One suspects that for many people the longing for a sense of participation is such that passages like this (and like the formulation that Christ is the Vine and we are the branches) have a strong appeal; and this may serve as partial explanation of the strong appeal that Vaughan's poems make to some readers (while admittedly leaving others unimpressed).

So far we have only looked at one example of what I have called a characteristic verbal progression. There are others! In 'Rules and Lessons' (lines 95–6) we read that *each tree, herb, flower/are shadows of his* wisdom, *and his power.* Here the sense of 'shadows' and the force of the rhyme ensure that the sense of individuality is, not obliterated, but subsumed into the higher sense of unity. In 'The Book', which in this connection warrants a full discussion, Vaughan writes *Thou knew'st this harmless* beast, *when he/Did live and feed by thy decree/On each green thing:* the linking by assonance of 'beast', 'he', 'feed', 'decree', 'each', and 'green' ensures our sense that the beast and each green thing live, and are related to each other, by God's decree.

There is another very clear example of such a verbal progression in the final poem in SILEX, the strongly eschatological 'L'Envoy':

Incline each hard heart to do good,
And cement us with thy son's blood,
That like true sheep, all in one fold
We may be fed, and one mind hold.

There is a more complex case in the same poem, in lines six to sixteen: it is as if Vaughan is saying that the tension between individuality and participation can only be resolved at the end, when the multiplicity of 'each' becomes the unity of 'all', vitrified to *a state/For evermore immaculate:*

Arise, arise!
And like old clothes fold up these skies,
This long worn veil: then shine and spread
Thy own bright self over each head,

And through thy creatures pierce and pass
Till all becomes thy cloudless glass,
Transparent as the purest day
And without blemish or decay,
Fixed by thy spirit to a state
For evermore immaculate.

I see 'The Book' as a hermetic poem because its assumption of an immortality for all living things and its very shape as a meditation are closely related to the hermetic tradition; part of its distinctiveness lies in its implication of the unity underlying Nature's diversity, and this too can be related to the thought of such sixteenth-century Nature-philosophers as Paracelsus and Agrippa. The actual *language* of the poem, its imagery, its strong pattern of assonance and rhyme, enact the sense of interdependence under God. To allow the reader to see this, and to deal with its themes properly, I shall quote the poem in full:

Eternal God! maker of all
That have lived here, since the man's fall;
The Rock of ages! in whose shade
They live unseen, when here they fade.

Thou knew'st this paper, *when it was*
Mere seed, *and after that but* grass;
Before 'twas dressed *or* spun, *and when*
Made linen, *who did* wear *it then:*
What were their lives, their thoughts & deeds
Whether good corn, *or fruitless* weeds.

Thou knew'st this tree, *when a green* shade
Covered it, since a cover *made,*

And where it flourished, grew and spread,
As if it never should be dead.

Thou knew'st this harmless beast, *when he*
Did live and feed by thy decree
On each green thing; then slept (well fed)
Clothed with this skin, *which now lies spread*
A covering *o'er this aged book,*
Which makes me wisely weep and look
On my own dust; mere dust it is,
But not so dry and clean as this.
Thou knew'st and saw'st them all and though
Now scattered thus, dost know them so.

O knowing, glorious spirit! when
Thou shalt restore trees, beasts and men,
When thou shalt make all new again,
Destroying only death and pain,
Give him amongst thy works a place,
Who in them loved and sought thy face!

This poem has no apparent difficulties of vocabulary or thought, and perhaps for that reason has received little attention from critics. Yet its quality invites attention; it is an impressive and characteristic poem, and one furthermore which (unlike other good poems of Vaughan's) has no very obvious relationship with biblical passages or the poems of George Herbert. It is patterned on the *meditation on the creatures* advocated in contemporary manuals of devotion; and in this of course it has affinities with other religious poems of the period, including others by Vaughan himself, for example 'Cock Crowing', 'The Bird', 'The Timber', and so on.

In this poem Vaughan strikes a distinctive note by meditating upon an artifact rather than upon a 'natural' object; but then he considers it, not as a man-made object, but rather as a coming-together of a number of natural elements. In the very process of Vaughan's thought here there is an implicit suggestion—that all man-made objects depend on the world given by God. The poet however does not make this explicit; profound as its implications may be, the thought itself was hardly daring or especially individual in the intellectual climate of that time. The poem moves rather towards a daring metaphysical statement; that 'trees' and 'beasts' are to be restored at the end, as well as men. This idea was not an accepted part of Western Christian orthodoxy. St. Thomas Aquinas had asserted that *dumb animals, plants and minerals . . . are corruptible . . . both on the part of their matter which loses its form, and on the part of their form which does not remain actually; and thus they are in no way subjects of incorruption. Hence, they will not remain in this renewal* (sc. 'at the last day').

The belief in the restitution of all things at the last day was a popular element in Renaissance hermeticism. Paracelsus asserted that all things *will reappear in the restitution,* Sir Thomas Browne forecast that at the last day God would command all things back into their proper shapes; and Pordage, in MUNDORUM EXPLICATIO, although asserting that the substance of things would perish, wrote that *the Forms shall remain unto Eternity,* which, if not as thoroughgoing as Browne, flatly contradicts Aquinas as quoted above. This belief in the final restitution of all things was of course an extension of the alchemists' theory of the transfiguration of all things, and hermetic mysticism as we have seen assumed the possibility of transfiguration in this life for true followers of Christ. This was not thought of as a purely 'subjective' experience: as Behmen had written, *Paradise . . . is in the world . . . swallowed up in the Mystery . . . but it is not altered in itself.* The convert, that is, is cleansed and strengthened in vision so that he is enabled to see what is actually there, but hidden from most men. The hermetists thought of the Paradise of God as offering a glorification of normal sense-experience: it is not likely that they should imagine a final bliss purged of the objects of sense.

'The Book' is marked by the tendency, not peculiar to the hermetists, but very strong among them, to see man as part of nature rather than as standing over and against Nature. The 'fade' of the fourth line is of course an echo of *all flesh is grass,* and the last line of the second stanza has an obvious source in the Gospels: but their effect in the poem is to play down the sense of the separateness of the various creatures, including man, from one another, and to endow them all with equality of status. We have soon forgotten that the book is an artifact, and are given a strong impression of God's world and the interdependence of its parts.

It is as if the *trees, beasts, and men* have been restored to life by Vaughan's imagination. A seventeenth-century specialist might experience 'The Book' as a poetic analogue of that hermetic experiment mentioned by Sir Thomas Browne in which the stock and the leaves of a plant are restored from its ashes. What is perhaps most important of all to note is that, in terms of hermetic thought, the metaphysical statement clearly implied by the final stanza, follows naturally and inescapably from the demonstrated imaginative process (the restoration of *trees, beasts, and men*) which precedes the final stanza. That is, in terms of hermetic thought, the last passage represents, not a mere poetic flight of fancy or wishful thinking but rather a conclusion logically earned.

The point lies in the status of imagination in hermetic epistemology. Paracelsus, Behmen and others of the time held the imagination in much higher esteem than it was to be held again before the time of the Romantic poets, who themselves, if recent scholarship is to be trusted, found intellectual support for their attitudes in the works of the Renaissance hermetists. Imagination for Hobbes was 'nothing but decaying sense'; but for Paracelsus it was creative, the magical intermediary between thought and being, which incarnates the thought in the image and brings the image into objective being. Moreover, Paracelsus thought that we could know about the creative processes of the deity by considering them analogically as a more potent version of our own creativity: the world exists as an exteriorisation of the imagination of God. Whereas man needs hands, and perhaps tools, to bring the content of his imagination into actual existence, God merely imagines, and wills, and the content of His imagination exists. So then, according to this mode of reasoning, this *religious way of knowing,* if Vaughan, by the imaginative contemplation of a man-made object, could recall the world of nature hidden within it, then God at the last day by an analogous process could restore all things from the dust.

'The Book' is a hermetic poem, in the sense that it belongs to one of those aspects of Christian doctrine which are as it were potential in the Bible, but not actualized in formal Christian theology, at any rate not in the west, and were taken up by Renaissance hermetic philosophers. However, the phraseology of the poem is not hermetic. There are no technical terms such as 'ray', 'tincture', 'signature', or 'magnetism', which in other poems point to the presence of hermetic notions.

It can hardly come as a surprise to his readers that Vaughan, who in so many poems *loved and sought God's face* in His works, was attracted by the doctrine of *the restitution of all things* as it was revived and developed by Renaissance hermetists. Such an idea, with its obvious emotional relationship with hermetic notions of transmutation and transfiguration, would obviously have a strong appeal and find a place in his eschatological themes. For his readers it is profoundly satisfying that an idea so consonant with Vaughan's love for God's creation should have found expression in so fine a poem as 'The Book'.

This poem, concerned as it is with the time *When thou shalt make all new again,/Destroying only death and pain* is clearly an eschatological work. Yet it is not directly concerned with any of the traditional four last things. In this chapter I have tried to show how Vaughan, in his eschatological thinking, is often most distinctively himself, and furthest away from the traditional orthodoxies. His most characteristic themes, of hiddenness, potentiality, transfiguration, multiplicity tending to unity, come together at this point. The magnificent urgency of Vaughan's language in his eschatological poems springs from his compelling need to find coherent meaning in a shattered world, from the need, that is, which led to the 'conversion' to which we owe SILEX SCINTILLANS.

Table of Dates

1621 Henry Vaughan and twin brother Thomas born at Newton-upon-Usk, Breconshire; probably the oldest surviving children of Thomas Vaughan of Tretower and Denise Morgan.

1628? William, their brother, born.

1632? Henry and Thomas Vaughan under the tuition of Matthew Herbert at Llangattock.

1638 *4 May.* Earliest evidence of Thomas Vaughan's residence at Jesus College, Oxford. It has been assumed that Henry went to Oxford at the same time, although there is no record of his residence there.

1640? Leaves Oxford for London to study Law.

1642? Returns to Breconshire as secretary to Judge Lloyd.

1646 Henry probably married (to Catherine Wise) by this date. He had a son, Thomas, and three daughters, Lucy, Frances and Catherine, by his first marriage. POEMS WITH THE TENTH SATIRE OF JUVENAL ENGLISHED published.

1647 17 *December.* Dedication of OLOR ISCANUS dated, more than three years before publication.

1648 *July*. William Vaughan dies.

1650 First part of SILEX SCINTILLANS published. Thomas evicted from his living at Llansantffraed.

1651 OLOR ISCANUS (poems with four prose translations) published. Registered April 28. *September*. Thomas Vaughan marries Rebecca (maiden name unknown).

1652 THE MOUNT OF OLIVES, OR SOLITARY DEVOTIONS published.

1653 13 *September*. Charles Walbeoffe dies, Vaughan's cousin, neighbour and close friend.

1654 FLORES SOLITUDINIS published.

1655 HERMETICAL PHYSIC published. Enlarged edition of SILEX SCINTILLANS published.

1655? Henry marries Elizabeth Wise, younger sister of his first wife. He had a son, Henry, and three daughters, Grisell, Lucy and Rachel, by his second marriage.

1657 THE CHEMIST'S KEY published.

1658 17 *April*. Rebecca, Thomas Vaughan's wife, dies. Thomas, Henry Vaughan's father, dies in early summer.

1660 Thomas Powell, neighbour and close friend, dies.

1661 Thomas Powell's HUMANE INDUSTRY published, containing some of Vaughan's verse translations.

1666 27 *February*. Thomas, Henry Vaughan's brother, dies at Albury, near Oxford.

1673 *June*. Beginning of the surviving correspondence between Henry Vaughan and John Aubrey, the biographer.

1678 THALIA REDIVIVA, containing poems by both Henry and Thomas, published.

1689 Henry and Elizabeth Vaughan move to a cottage in Scethrog to vacate the house at Newton, where he was born and lived for most of his life, in favour of Thomas, Henry's son by his first marriage.

1695 23 *April*. Henry Vaughan dies. Buried in Llansantffraed churchyard.

Bibliography

Editions

Alexander B. Grosart, THE WORKS IN VERSE AND PROSE COMPLETE OF HENRY VAUGHAN, SILURIST, FOR THE FIRST TIME COLLECTED AND EDITED: WITH MEMORIAL INTRODUCTION: ESSAY ON LIFE AND WRITING, The Fuller Worthies' Library, 1871.

E. K. Chambers, THE POEMS OF HENRY VAUGHAN, Lawrence & Bullen, London and Charles Scribner's Sons, New York, 2 vols., 1896.

L. C. Martin, THE WORKS OF HENRY VAUGHAN, Oxford University Press, 1914; second edn., 1957.

E. L. Marilla, THE SECULAR POEMS OF HENRY VAUGHAN, Essays and Studies on English Language and Literature XXI, Uppsala, Harvard and Copenhagen, 1958.

French Fogle, THE COMPLETE POETRY OF HENRY VAUGHAN, Doubleday & Co., New York, 1964; Norton, New York, 1969.

Christopher Dixon, A SELECTION FROM HENRY VAUGHAN, Longman, 1967.

Alan Rudrum, HENRY VAUGHAN: THE COMPLETE POEMS, Penguin, London, 1976.

Bibliographies and Concordances

Robert E. Bourdette, Jr, 'Recent Studies in Henry Vaughan', ENGLISH LITERARY RENAISSANCE, IV no. 2 (1974), pp. 299–310.

E. L. Marilla, A COMPREHENSIVE BIBLIOGRAPHY OF HENRY VAUGHAN, University of Alabama Studies, no. 3, 1948.

E. L. Marilla and James D. Simmonds, HENRY VAUGHAN: A BIBLIOGRAPHICAL SUPPLEMENT, 1946–1960, University of Alabama Studies, no. 16, 1963.

Imilda Tuttle, CONCORDANCE TO VAUGHAN'S SILEX SCINTILLANS, Pennsylvania State University Press, Pittsburgh, 1969.

Biography

F. E. Hutchinson, HENRY VAUGHAN: A LIFE AND INTERPRETATION, The Clarendon Press, 1947; reprinted 1962; corrected reprint 1971.

Selected Critical Studies

Don Cameron Allen (ed.), 'Henry Vaughan: "Cock Crowing" ', in IMAGE AND MEANING: METAPHORIC TRADITIONS IN RENAISSANCE POETRY, Johns Hopkins University Press, Baltimore, 1960, pp. 154–69.

S. L. Bethell, THE CULTURAL REVOLUTION OF THE SEVENTEENTH CENTURY, Dobson, 1951.

Edmund Blunden, ON THE POEMS OF HENRY VAUGHAN, Richard Cobden-Sanderson, 1927.

A. U. Chapman, 'Henry Vaughan and magnetic philosophy', SOUTHERN REVIEW (Adelaide), IV, iii (1971), pp. 215–26.

Wilson O. Clough, 'Henry Vaughan and the hermetic philosophy', PUBLICATIONS OF THE MODERN LANGUAGE ASSOCIATION OF AMERICA, XLVIII (1933), pp. 1108–1130.

Robert Allen Durr, ON THE MYSTICAL POETRY OF HENRY VAUGHAN, Harvard University Press, 1962.

Kenneth Friedenreich, HENRY VAUGHAN, Boston, Mass., 1978.

Ross Garner, HENRY VAUGHAN: EXPERIENCE AND THE TRADITION, University of Chicago Press, 1959.

Elizabeth Holmes, HENRY VAUGHAN AND THE HERMETIC PHILOSOPHY, Blackwell, 1932.

Merritt Y. Hughes, 'The theme of pre-existence and infancy in "The Retreat", PHILOLOGICAL QUARTERLY, XX (1941), pp. 484–500, reprinted in Baldwin Maxwell *et al.*, RENAISSANCE STUDIES IN HONOR OF HARDIN CRAIG, Folcroft, Stanford, 1941, pp. 292–308.

A. C. Judson, 'The Source of Henry Vaughan's ideas concerning God in Nature', STUDIES IN PHILOLOGY, XXIV (1927), pp. 592–606.

Frank Kermode, 'The private imagery of Henry Vaughan', REVIEW OF ENGLISH STUDIES, New Series, 1 (1950), pp. 206–25.

Margherita Leardi, LA POESIA DI HENRY VAUGHAN, La Nuova Italia Editrice, Florence, 1967.

M. M. Mahood, POETRY AND HUMANISM, Cape, 1950; corrected edn., Norton, New York, 1970.

L. C. Martin, 'Henry Vaughan and the theme of infancy', in John Purves (ed.) SEVENTEENTH CENTURY STUDIES PRESENTED TO SIR HERBERT GRIERSON, The Clarendon Press, 1938, pp. 243–55.

L. C. Martin, 'Henry Vaughan and "Hermes Trismegistus" ', REVIEW OF ENGLISH STUDIES, XVIII (1942), pp. 301–307.

Louis L. Martz, THE POETRY OF MEDITATION, Yale University Press and Oxford University Press, 1954.

Louis L. Martz, THE PARADISE WITHIN, Yale University Press, 1964.

Earl Miner, THE METAPHYSICAL MODE FROM DONNE TO COWLEY, Princeton University Press, 1969.

William R. Parker, 'Henry Vaughan and his publishers', THE LIBRARY, 4th series, XX (1940), pp. 401–11.

E. C. Pettet, OF PARADISE AND LIGHT: A STUDY OF VAUGHAN'S SILEX SCINTILLANS, Cambridge University Press, 1960.

Jonathan F. S. Post, 'Vaughan's "The Night" and his "late and dusky" Age', STUDIES IN ENGLISH LITERATURE, 19 (1979), pp. 127–141.

Maren-Sofie Røstvig, THE HAPPY MAN, STUDIES IN THE METAMORPHOSES OF A CLASSICAL IDEAL, vol. 1, Universitetsforlaget, Oslo and Blackwell, 1954; vol. 2, Universitetsforlaget, Oslo and Blackwell, 1958.

A. W. Rudrum, 'Henry Vaughan's "The Book": a hermetic poem', JOURNAL OF THE AUSTRALASIAN UNIVERSITIES LANGUAGE AND LITERATURE ASSOCIATION (1961), pp. 161–6.

A. W. Rudrum, 'Henry Vaughan and the theme of transfiguration', SOUTHERN REVIEW (Adelaide), I (1963), pp. 54–68.

A. W. Rudrum, 'Vaughan's "The Night": some hermetic notes', MODERN LANGUAGE REVIEW, LXIV (1969), pp. 11–19.

Alan Rudrum, 'Vaughan's "Each"', ESSAYS IN CRITICISM, 21, No. 1 (1971), pp. 86–91.

James D. Simmonds, 'Vaughan's "The Book": hermetic or meditative', NEOPHILOLOGUS, XLVII (1963) pp. 320–8.

James D. Simmonds, MASQUES OF GOD: FORM AND THEME IN THE POETRY OF HENRY VAUGHAN, University of Pittsburgh Press, 1972.

Arthur J. M. Smith, 'Some relations between Henry Vaughan and Thomas Vaughan', PAPERS

OF THE MICHIGAN ACADEMY OF SCIENCE, ARTS, AND LETTERS, XVIII (1933), pp. 551–61.

Bain Tate Stewart, 'Hermetic symbolism in Henry Vaughan's "The Night" ', PHILOLOGICAL QUARTERLY, XXIX (1950), pp. 417–22.

Joseph H. Summers, THE HEIRS OF DONNE AND JONSON, Chatto & Windus, 1970.

Harold R. Walley, 'The strange case of OLOR ISCANUS', REVIEW OF ENGLISH STUDIES, XVIII (1942), pp. 27–37.

R. H. Walters, 'Henry Vaughan and the alchemists', REVIEW OF ENGLISH STUDIES, XXIII (1947), pp. 107–22.

R. M. Wardle, 'Thomas Vaughan's influence upon the poetry of Henry Vaughan', PUBLICATIONS OF THE MODERN LANGUAGE ASSOCIATION OF AMERICA, LI (1936), pp. 936–52.

Helen C. White, THE METAPHYSICAL POETS, Macmillan, 1936.

Abbreviations

POEMS Alan Rudrum, HENRY VAUGHAN: THE COMPLETE POEMS, Penguin, London, 1976.

M L. C. Martin, THE WORKS OF HENRY VAUGHAN, Oxford University Press, 1914; second edn, 1957.

LIFE F. E. Hutchinson, HENRY VAUGHAN: A LIFE AND INTERPRETATION, The Clarendon Press, 1947; reprinted 1962; corrected reprint 1971.

A Note on Quotations

Except in one instance, where the reason will be obvious, quotations from Vaughan's poems are taken from the present author's edition.

Acknowledgements

An earlier version of the section on Vaughan's secular poems appeared in POETRY WALES, and I am grateful for permission to use it here. I have also drawn occasionally upon my earlier publications on Vaughan, especially an article on 'The Book', which first appeared in AUMLA, and a titled review which first appeared in ESSAYS in CRITICISM, 'Vaughan's "Each"'.

I wish to thank June Sturrock, who read the entire work and made many useful suggestions; Eileen Stevens, of the Dean of Arts' Office, Simon Fraser University, who cleared my path on several occasions; Bernice Ferrier, Penny McLaren and Elsie Trott, who typed this essay; Dr. R. C. Brown, the Dean of Arts, who gave a grant-in-aid; and Marjorie Weir, who corrected typographical errors and castigated convoluted sentences. Such errors and infelicities as remain are my own.

The Author

Alan Rudrum has been Professor of English at Simon Fraser University, British Columbia, since 1969. Born at Great Yarmouth in 1932, he was educated at Doncaster Grammar School and the Universities of London, Cambridge and Nottingham. He has published widely, mostly on the religious verse of seventeenth-century England.

This Edition
designed by Jeff Clements,
is set in Monotype Spectrum 12 Didot on 13 point
and printed on Basingwerk Parchment by
Qualitex Printing Limited, Cardiff

It is limited to 1000 copies of which this is

Copy No. 385

British Library Cataloguing in Publication Data

Rudrum, Alan

Henry Vaughan — (Writers of Wales,
ISSN 0141–5050)
1. Vaughan, Henry — Criticism and interpretation
I. Series
821'.4 PR3743

ISBN 0–7083–0787–6

DATE DU

PRINTED IN U.S.A.

GAYLORD